Ultralight Spin-Fishing

A Practical Guide for Freshwater & Saltwater Anglers

Ultralight Spin-Fishing

A Practical Guide for
Freshwater & Saltwater Anglers

Peter F. Cammann

The Countryman Press
Woodstock, Vermont

©1994 by Peter F. Cammann

Library of Congress Cataloging-in-Publication Data

Cammann, Peter F., 1957-
Ultralight spin-fishing: a practical guide for freshwater & saltwater anglers / Peter F. Cammann
  p. cm.
Includes index.
ISBN 0-88150-301-0
1. Spin-fishing.   I. Title.
SH456.5.C36 1994
799.1'2 — dc20   94-26283
                                                        CIP

Published by The Countryman Press, Inc.
Woodstock, VT 05091

Cover design by Leslie Carlson
Cover photograph by Mike Barlow
Text design by Karen Savary
Interior photographs by the author unless otherwise credited
Line art for Chapter 8 ©1994 by Patti Zimmerman, Wisteria Graphics
Knot diagrams in Chapter 5 provided by Stren® Fishing Lines
Line art in Chapter 7 provided by O. Mustad and Son (USA), Inc.

Printed in the United States of America
10 9 8 7 6 5 4 3 2 1

For Grace

Contents

Acknowledgments

When I first began writing this book, the words of an old friend came to mind:

"If you thought writing your first book was tough, just wait until you start your second. One day you'll wake up and say to yourself, 'Good God! I can't possibly do all of this again.'" Writing this book was hard, harder than anything else I've done in my life, except perhaps the day-to-day struggle of trying to be a good husband to my wife, Lauren, and a good father to my daughter, Grace. But, like living with the two women in my life, it has also been a fabulous experience, one I would never wish to trade.

Part of the reward in writing a book like this has been working with the many fine people who helped me along my way. I received extraordinary cooperation from the many manufacturers of ultralight spinning tackle described in these pages. I would also like to thank Joe Kuti of the American Fishing Tackle Manufacturers Association for helping me to define the scope of this project. Jerry Gibbs of *Outdoor Life* magazine was a great help in preparing the chapter on fishing lines and always offered his encouragement, for which I am extremely grateful. I also must thank my good friend Rob Scharges for heading out onto the water with me to research the various products and fish species discussed. It's always nice to know that there are other people besides me who will use any excuse to go fishing.

I have to acknowledge all of the support I received from the good people at Countryman Press. Carl Taylor is really the man behind the idea for this book, and I thank him for suggesting it. I was very lucky to have his advice throughout this project and the benefit of his skills as editor. I was also fortunate to have Castle Freeman as an editor and am thankful to him for tightening up the final manuscript. Michael Gray was responsible for overseeing the designing of the attractive package for this book. Also, many thanks to Bob Mastejulia and Sonja Hakala for their efforts in marketing the final product.

Finally, I would like to thank you, the reader, for buying this book. You're really the one who made all this possible. Keep in touch and let me know how you do on the water.

An Introduction to Ultralight Fishing

I t wasn't until the summer of 1987 that I first went fishing for trout without my fly rod. I always assumed that these most noble of freshwater game fish were meant to be taken on the traditional gear of Izaak Walton, Ernest Hemingway, and Lefty Kreh. For close to twenty years, I had labored under the illusion that to fish correctly, *one must fish with a fly*, preferably a dry-hackled one.

Well, that one summer managed to undo a lifetime of misconceptions. I still fish with flies almost everywhere I go, from the cool, clean rivers of Vermont to the open seas of the Atlantic and the Caribbean. However, I now pack along an ultralight spinning rod too and have found that it has opened up dozens of new and exciting possibilities for each place I visit. Ultralight is not a new sport but a variation on the time-honored kit of the spinning angler. Over the past five years or so, however, ultralight has seen enormous growth within the fishing tackle market and has gained enthusiasts from all over the world.

As a fishing guide, I watched the huge explosion in the fly-fishing market during the 1980s as weekend anglers took to the sport by the thousands. These folks would show up to fish with me, bringing with them the very best equipment that money could buy, and more often than not little understanding of how to use any of it. I admired their enthusiasm, though, as they lashed away at the water, often terrifying all of the fish within earshot.

But as the '80s came to a close and we entered the more uncertain economic climate of this decade, I noticed that more and more of my clients were coming to me with ultralight gear. These small, relatively inexpensive rods and reels and tiny lures were becoming the order of the day, and I had to make some adjustments to cope with them and their owners.

The ultralight angler, like the fly-fisherman, is a devotee of the belief that smaller is better. While ultralight equipment is not exactly a new development in spin-fishing (it has existed for many decades now), its newly found popularity is in part explained by the unique challenge to the angler of using this downsized gear.

Fishing is a great sport because you will spend your entire life learning more about it. Ultralight offers the challenge of taking good-sized fish on extremely light tackle and also affords you a much better opportunity for observing fish while you do so than you would have with conventional spinning gear. As in fly-fishing, the secret to ultralight is your ability to fool the fish entirely by sight or motion. You are using very small lures, and the extra stealth afforded you by small lures and almost invisible light lines means you should be able to sneak up on schooling fish more effectively than you can when you use heavier gear. While using ultralight gear, I have had great fun watching barracuda feed, for instance, or bass spawn, because the fish simply did not know I was there observing them. Each fishing trip, then, brings a double dividend when you use ultralight: (1) the thrill of a great fight; and (2) the information obtained by being in such close proximity to your quarry.

Ultralight combines the touch of fly-fishing with the high technology of modern spin-angling. Despite the fact that it is in some ways similar to both of these styles of fishing, however, it is also quite distinct from either. You cannot cast a fly with a standard spinning rod, but you can with an ultralight. You might be limited in your ability to cast into a brushy stream with a fly rod, but you will not be with an ultralight rod. By combining the best of these two traditions, ultralight fishing is now creating one of its own.

Ultralight means exactly what it sounds like: extremely lightweight spinning equipment used to fish with lures that weigh anywhere from ¹⁄₁₀₀ to ¼ ounce. In fact, a ¼-ounce lure is considered almost to be overkill by the devotees of this sport, and they will use lures in this size only for the very largest of fish.

The lines associated with ultralight are interesting, too, and manufacturers have rushed to develop them in 1- through 6-pound tests to meet the growing demand. Most ultralight anglers seem to prefer the middle range of 4-pound test, but others swear that the challenge of fishing with 2-pound cannot be beaten. I have fished for saltwater species like barracuda and bluefish with 5- and 6-pound line, though, and I can promise you that the extra strength in my line was of fairly small comfort when dealing with these hearty species.

In the end, the real thrill for the ultralight angler is in using your wits and the full measure of your abilities to take a fish without injuring it or damaging your equipment. To illustrate the excitement involved, let me tell you a story about a good friend of mine who uses light gear to angle for just about every species of fish. Several years ago we took a fabulous trip to the Massachusetts coast.

In October of 1986, I was asked by Jerry McKinnis, host and producer of the ESPN cable television program "The Fishin' Hole" to guide a bluefish trip for his show. Since I lived most of my life in the coastal towns of Massachusetts and New York, much of the fishing I did as a child was on the ocean. A good deal of that angling experience was spent surfcasting for bluefish, and so my favored gear for these fish was the surfcaster's standard: an 8- or 10-foot fiberglass rod of medium stiffness, a heavy-duty 16-ounce open-face spinning reel, and 12-pound test monofilament line. Even if you use this rugged gear, a bluefish can exact a terrible toll. They are extremely powerful fish with a talent for straining line and tackle.

Jerry, on the other hand, is a resident of Arkansas, originally from Missouri. His experience, which is extraordinary, has lead him to the conclusion that most fish can be taken with the very lightest of graphite rods, small reels, and 4- or 6-pound-test line. He has fished all over the world with this kind of rig—and with enormous success, as his weekly television show attests. Both he and his cameraman, Mark DeLinde, kidded me about the size of my boat rod and surfcasting rig, asking whether I intended on catching fish or beating them to death. While I also had used fly gear for schoolies (small striped bass) and snappers, up until this particular trip I had always sided with caution in dealing with adult blues and used heavier gear.

In any case, back to Jerry, his tiny rod and reel, and the many 5- to 12-pound bluefish he caught on our trip. It was an incredible experience to watch him work a fish in. As one good 10-pound blue he hooked leaped toward the boat and shook its

Ultralight gear makes it possible to take a rod along almost any-where and enjoy the outdoors.

head in an attempt to throw the hook, Jerry applied pressure to the oncoming fish, anticipating the move. When the fish dove, he swung his rod downward and to the side, keeping the pressure on without overly straining his thin line. As the fish rose again and jumped with a twisting motion away from the boat, Jerry quickly back-reeled to allow the fish to run while he continued to apply pressure and maintain control of the fight.

I was fascinated. This guy had taken a good-sized blue on gear I wouldn't even have used for trout back home in Vermont. The following season, I started using ultralight equipment on some of my favorite Vermont trout rivers, with some fantastic results. The light line was very effective in helping me fool trout, especially during those bright days when the water ran clear and the fish were easily spooked. It reminded me at first of fishing with my fly rod and using a long 7X (2-pound-test) leader tippet. The principle was the same. You use an extra-light tippet to blend in with the surroundings, allowing the fish to be attracted by what appears to be a natural fly floating on the water. The ultralight lines I used that summer, all in the 2- and 4-pound-test range, gave me enormous versatility in placing small ⅛-ounce and 1⁄12-ounce lures right into pools of fish without arousing their suspicion. The minimal wind resistance which these light lines encounter also increased the accuracy of my casts, especially casting into the wind.

I also got a big kick out of how responsive the ultralight rods were. A short rod does not mean a short cast, I discovered, nor does it limit the size of fish you may pursue with it. These tough graphite rods are built to take enormous stress and still provide you with enough flex that you can feel even the lightest strike. The reels astonished me with how highly geared they are, giving me the ability to bring in line to keep up with fish as they charged straight at me. The drags on the reels are also strong enough to handle hard-running fish and to help you meet a wide variety of water conditions.

Remember: the first big advantage that ultralight gear affords you is sensitivity. Like the tip of a fly rod, the ultralight rod tip flexes easily, allowing you to feel strikes which might otherwise have gone undetected. The lightweight line helps to this end as well, compounding your advantage. If you can feel a fish as it lightly inhales your lure, you have a far better chance of connecting on that strike. Smallmouth bass, for example, will strike at a jig with a light action, which feels like a little *tick* at the end of your line. A heavy monofilament will mask this slight action, making it difficult for you to even know the fish is there. Equally sensitive are the small reels used in ultralight spin-fishing, which are specifically designed to work with the short rods and light lines you are going to use. They are very light, too, which will give you an even better feel of your line and of the play in your rod.

The second big advantage to ultralight gear is control. Ultralight allows you to exert great control over the fish you are fighting and to monitor how that fish is faring, and the small lures, like flies, increase the likelihood that a fish will survive if released. I am a great believer in the philosophy of catch-and-release fishing, the concept that we should release as many fish as possible each time we go out, to insure the future of this great sport.

I read an interesting article in the *USA Today* sports section on the dwindling catches of bluefish off the East Coast. It seems that recreational fishing catches came in at nineteen million in 1989, up from sixteen million the year before. While that sounds like an awful lot of fish, keep in mind that in the period between 1979 and 1987 anglers *averaged* thirty-one million blues each season. If you consider that anglers each season take thirty million trips out to catch bluefish, it means that the daily average had slipped from a shade over one fish per trip to about half that in just two years.

States along the Atlantic Coast have been working to reverse this trend, many of them by adopting new size restrictions and limits to keep the annual kill down. Some have enacted legislation which imposes a ten-fish limit on blues, while others have tied their limits to size restrictions. These laws only govern angling activities from the shoreline out to 3 miles offshore. From 3 miles out to the 200-mile limit, the U.S. Commerce Department has jurisdiction, and in May of 1990, the department enacted a management plan which sets a ten-fish limit on all recreational anglers fishing in federal waters from Maine to Florida.

This was all encouraging news, as it marked one of the first times that state and federal governments have worked to actively prevent the depletion of a fish species *before* that species began to suffer a sharp drop-off in its numbers. Perhaps you remember the scrambling which took place at the state and federal level during the mid-eighties when it appeared that the striped bass was becoming an endangered species. The drastic measures taken at that time did indeed prove successful, but we came dangerously close to losing this fine game fish for good.

What does all this have to do with us and the sport of ultralight fishing? Quite a lot. You see, we have our own wild populations of game fish to manage in inland states, and there's a lot more we could be doing toward that end. If there's a lesson to be learned from the bluefish and the striped bass, it is that no species exists in an inexhaustible supply from which we may harvest thoughtlessly. Trout, bass, and panfish, like the bluefish in the Atlantic Ocean, are a long way away from being endangered species, but it's never too early to consider what it would be like if one day they did begin to disappear from our neighborhood fishing holes, and it's never too early to reflect on what we might do now to keep that day from coming.

Using This Book

In chapter 2, "Buying Your Equipment," we'll look at how to best take advantage of the knowledge which a good tackle shop can offer you in buying your ultralight rig. This chapter will offer you information on how to deal with salespeople and purchase the equipment that is right for you.

Chapter 3, "The Rods," will describe the ultralight rod in detail: its size, its action, its manufacture, its use, and other topics, including information on what several manufacturers are now offering.

In chapter 4, "The Reels," we get into gear ratios, reel weights, "quick fire" triggers, front or rear drag controls. What's an angler to do? This chapter will explain the relative advantages and disadvantages of these and other options as well as provide a review of what's out in the marketplace in the way of open-face, ultralight reels.

Chapter 5, "The Line," asks the question: Why get excited about plain old fishing line? Because there are so many lines now on the market, and most of them do very different things. There are lines designed for light weight, limpness, stretch, strength under pressure, salt water, fresh water, etc. All have unique advantages and disadvantages which we will review.

Chapter 6, "The Lures," discusses floating plugs, diving crankbaits, jigs, spoons, spinners—all of which are designed by manufacturers to act differently in the water. They also are often designed to catch specific kinds of fish.

Chapter 7, "Gadgets and Gizmos": This is the fun chapter of the book. Everything from surgical forceps to stream thermometers will get a once-over as we look at all of the peripheral toys associated with ultralight.

In chapter 8, "Casting," we'll see that long casts are a good thing for the ultralight angler stalking a wary brown trout lying in the flat but are less important for catching a brook trout that has pushed itself up against a cut bank on a small stream. This chapter will detail flipping, backhand, and sidearm casting as well as other techniques for fishing in tight quarters.

Chapters 9 through 14 will offer you precise information on how to use ultralight equipment to catch various species of fish. While most of this part of the book will be devoted to freshwater species like trout, salmon, bass, pike, and panfish, I'll also be telling you more about how to use these small rigs on saltwater fish.

I hope you will enjoy this book. I had a lot of fun putting it together for you. It has allowed me to spend time playing in oceans, streams, and lakes with my ultralight gear. For this, I thank you.

ONE

The Gear and Its Use

2

Buying Your Equipment

Anyone who has wandered into a tackle shop or thumbed through the pages of a fishing catalogue will understand it when I tell you: there are so many choices out there in the marketplace of fishing equipment that you can be left in a state of total paralysis trying to figure out what to get. Fishing is a huge industry, responsible for billions of dollars in sales and support services. Roughly one out every four Americans goes fishing at least once every year, and that means that the manufacturers of fishing equipment are aiming at an extremely broad-based market in their attempts to sell their products.

In spite of this, fishing tackle manufacturing has become a more and more compartmentalized and specialized industry. Because the sheer numbers of anglers reflect the broad diversity of American life, varying tastes have forced the industry to offer an almost endlessly increasing variety of ways for anglers to spend their money. The problem for the angler is not whether there is a choice to make, but how to make the best choice.

Purchasing a piece of fishing equipment is as personal a decision as what clothes to wear, what music to listen to, or what kind of home to live in. It is not easy, either. In order to choose what is appropriate for your needs, you need to do research. In fact, you should begin that research process before you even set foot in a tackle shop or call an 800 number to see what is for sale in a catalogue.

The Importance of Balance

In the chapters on rods and reels, you will read how important it is to buy a combo that is balanced. A balanced rod/reel is easy to check for and extremely important to the success of your fishing trips. First, let us look at why balance is an issue at all.

For you to efficiently cast your line, your rod and reel must match each other. You would never take a 1-pound surfcasting reel and put it on a 4½-foot ultralight rod, because you would be unable to cast with that combination. The huge reel would be constantly fouling as it attempted to load more line than your small rod was capable of handling each time you took a cast. On the other hand, it would be just as inappropriate to slap an ultralight reel on an 8-foot boat rod. The reel would be unable to load the larger, stiff-action rod effectively.

So, when looking at ultralight rods and reels, be mindful that while the illustrations I have just offered are laughably exaggerated, the same principles apply in real life. Do not buy a reel and rod that are not matched to each other, as you will just be purchasing an endless string of headaches for yourself once you start using them. Instead, take a few minutes out while you are browsing and test a few rods and reels for compatibility.

Slap a reel onto a rod and hold the rod gently by your thumb and forefinger just above where the reel is mounted. If the rod and reel match each other in weight, the rod tip will balance parallel to the floor. If the reel is too heavy, the tip will rise, and if it is too light, the tip will tilt downward. Once you find a rod and reel that balance out, your next step should be to see how they cast together.

Exploring Options at Expositions

Every winter there are dozens of regional fishing and hunting expositions held at civic auditoriums throughout the country.

These trade shows are perhaps the best research resource for the angler trying to narrow down his or her equipment choices. Hundreds of products are on display at these expos, and manufacturers' representatives are there, eager to answer questions about their wares. Even better, there are often opportunities at these shows to actually test the products you see before buying them.

At most of the larger expos, you will find a shallow casting pool where many of the celebrity anglers who frequent the shows deliver their lectures. During the dead time in between lectures, the casting pool is available to you for testing the equipment displayed at the expo. You can learn a lot in a very short period of time by taking advantage of this.

One February I found myself at an expo in Worcester, Massachusetts, working with the Vermont Fish and Wildlife Department to promote fishing in that state. I took a one-hour break and went to visit a few of the exhibits with the idea of perhaps buying a new rod and reel for myself. I went over to one of the booths and asked if I could get a rod and reel to test out. The salesman handed me a setup, and I wandered over to the cast-

A balanced rod and reel combination is easy to check and extremely important to your fishing success

ing pool. I discovered that while I loved the reel I had been given, I was not happy with the way it felt on the rod it had been matched with. An important piece of information had been gained, because I now knew which reel I wanted. I went back to the same booth, tested a few more rod and reel combinations, and found another reel and a rod that impressed me. All in all, this had been a very productive half-hour.

I then visited several more booths, testing rods and reels and eliminating the ones that did not suit me. While I did not make any purchases that day, I learned a lot about the various types of gear available and was then able to make my next purchase having been well educated at the expo by the sales reps there and by working the casting pool on my own.

Selecting a Tackle Shop

As your research into ultralight equipment continues, your next step might be to visit a few tackle shops to find what real prices are. At most expos, the salespeople will be selling the product for full retail. This is particularly true if you visit a booth where the tackle manufacturer is represented. Manufacturers usually agree to sell their gear to the public at the full retail price so retailers can offer discounts to the public at their shops. After all, the manufacturer makes his margin by selling to wholesale distributors who then sell to the retail stores who in turn make the final sales to consumers. In order to make both the wholesale distributor and the retailer happy, the manufacturer agrees that his price will always be the highest possible should he ever sell directly to the public, as at expos. It therefore makes very little sense for you as the consumer to ever buy directly from the manufacturer, as you will probably be paying more than you would if you went through a retailer who is free to set his own price.

The advantages of buying from a retailer are, however, becoming somewhat less pronounced. More and more now, manufacturers are mandating that retailers sell their gear at the suggested retail price, or at a minimum price above wholesale cost. This is an attempt by the manufacturers to prevent the larger discount stores and mail-order catalogues from wiping out their small store competition by offering gear at a loss. The loss leader has been a powerful weapon of the chain stores for decades, as it lures consumers with specially priced items which smaller stores cannot offer at the same price. A larger firm can afford to sustain short-term losses on a few items in this way because the profit derived from the increased consumer traffic and subsequent sales will more than make up for them. Big stores also know that the loss in revenue to the smaller retailer may drive him out of business, thereby opening up new markets to the larger stores as the bankrupt store's customers look for new places to shop. Equipment manufacturers can ill afford to lose retail outlets, either large or small, for their goods in this highly competitive marketplace, and so they are working to bring prices into some kind of balance through mandated retail pricing. Still, even with minimum pricing, you should be able to ferret out some bargains by looking carefully at what is available in retail stores and in catalogues.

While it is often easier to check prices through a mail-order catalogue, there are some big advantages to doing your window shopping at a retail store. To begin with, you will be able to draw on the experience of the sales personnel. Most tackle shops are owned by people who got into the business because they love to fish. This means they will be apt to have answers when you ask how a certain reel works with a certain rod. More importantly, these folks are also likely to know which lures are most effective in local waters. The information you can gather from talking with a tackle shop owner on lures, local fishing conditions, and even the names of qualified guides in the area can make the visit more than worthwhile by itself.

A word of caution about buying your gear at large department stores. From time to time, you will read about big clearance sales being held in shopping mall department stores. "Everything's Gotta Go!" is an advertising phrase designed to make even the most cautious bargain hunter salivate with anticipation. And quite often you can find good deals at mall stores. I do feel, however, that the one great disadvantage to buying your tackle at big department stores—huge megaplexes that carry everything from toasters to bowling balls—is that the salespeople there are not apt to be as knowledgeable as the ones you will find at small local tackle shops. If you do decide to buy at a mall, be sure to educate yourself on the gear you are looking for before you step inside.

Warranties

In addition to looking at prices, you should be asking questions about warranties. Warranties are always set by the manufacturers, but it is usually the retailer with whom you will have to deal should you have a problem with your newly purchased equipment. Some retailers are very accommodating and will offer to exchange equipment damaged under the warranty with gear right out of their stock. There is no real reason why shops should not do this, either, as in most cases the manufacturer will simply reimburse the retailer for all defective equipment when the retailer places his next order and sends back the damaged goods he has received. There are, however, exceptions to this rule, and you should be on the lookout for them.

I was guiding a client on a trout fishing trip when his fishing rod suddenly snapped in two during a cast. Since we were nearly at the end of the tour, we decided to hang it up and hike back to where I had parked my truck. We drove over to my office, and I had the client call up the tackle shop where he bought the rod, which was only about a half-hour's drive away. To our amazement, the manager of the shop told my client that he was not responsible for warranty work and that in order to get satisfaction, he would have to take the matter up with the manufacturer.

I sold the same rod through my mail-order catalogue at the time, and so we called the manufacturer and spoke to a service representative at the plant. The service representative seemed confused by our story and told us that if we would have the shop manager call her, she would assure him that the factory would indeed honor the warranty. She added that she did not understand what the problem was, as all retailers of that particular rod had been told that exchanges for defective gear under warranty were automatically honored by her company. We finally heard from the store manager, and my client was told to drive over and exchange his broken rod for a new one, but that happy ending was not without delay, frustration, and disappointment.

This story should stress to you the importance of finding out ahead of time where a retailer stands when it comes to taking care of you after the sale. You should also be just as careful in this respect when checking out mail-order catalogues. With catalogue companies, you should try to find out whether you or they are responsible for the charges associated with shipping damaged equipment back under warranty. You should also find out whether the mail-order firm requires that you call in advance of returning broken equipment and if you are required to get a Merchandise Return Authorization number (MRA). Quite a few catalogue companies will not accept returns without the MRA. In all cases, whether you are dealing with a shop or a catalogue company, find out if they plan to attempt to repair the broken equipment or if they will replace it with a new item from stock. Repair work can take several weeks or even months, which can be inconvenient during the middle of fishing season.

Working with Salespeople

The salesperson is in many ways the most important link in your search for the right ultralight rig for yourself. As I have mentioned, a good salesman can be valuable in terms of the information he may be able to offer you about the lines he carries, and by and large, the salespeople in tackle shops are knowledgeable and helpful. A poor salesman is a problem, though, and you should be alert to the possibility of running into one.

Poor salespeople are not evil or greedy. In fact, many of the worst salespeople I have come across in my experience were as well intentioned, honest, and outgoing as any of the good ones. What separates good from bad here is knowledge—or the lack of it. A good salesman will make himself known to you through the information he peddles as well as the quality of merchandise he stocks. If you walk into a store with well-stocked racks and shelves, offering a wide variety of goods covering a broad price range, you probably have stumbled upon a good shop. Do not be confused or overly impressed with flashy overhead lighting, big displays, or walls filled with clearance-sale-priced items. Some of the best shops I have found are dark, a little dingy, but filled with all the gear you would ever hope to own. Look for variety as your first clue to whether a shop is any good.

Second, ask lots of questions. I find it useful to ask a question that I already know the answer to, just to get a feel for the knowledge that a given salesperson might have. I also want to know if he is listening or if he is just thinking of gear he can sell me. Sometimes I will tell a salesperson that I am looking for a rod or a reel and then describe the characteristics of one that I own and like very much. If the salesperson directs me to the equipment I already own, or a reasonable alternative, I know he is listening to my needs and also knows his equipment. If the salesperson can show me that he knows his stuff and is truly interested in getting me the gear I say I need, then I have found someone I can do business with.

Get a feel for prices before you buy. You can spend an enormous amount of money on your ultralight rig if that is what makes you happy, or you can cut a few costs and buy something in a lower price range to fit your budget. For a well-built, inexpensive rod and reel, you can expect to pay $50–$70. If you decide you want something a little flashier, a rod built from a better blank or a reel with a few more bells and whistles on it, get ready to spend all the way up to $200 or even more. My favorite ultralight rig cost me just about $100 when I bought it in 1991.

Once you have ascertained what you want to buy and have found the right price and service agreement for your needs, it is time to break out the wallet and plunk down the cash. In the next five chapters, we will cover the various types of rods, reels, lines, lures, and other gadgets that are out there to choose from.

3
The Rods

The selection of an ultralight fishing rod is one of the most personal decisions any angler has to make. If you follow a few simple rules of thumb, your search for the right fishing rod or rods for your purposes will be significantly simpler.

Action

Unlike fly-fishing, where rods are described in terms of their weight (meaning what weight line is appropriate for any given rod), length, and action, ultralight rods are only discussed in respect to length and action. "Ultralight" is a standard term, as I explained in chapter 1, describing a style of extremely lightweight spinning tackle. All of the rods we will take up in this chapter fall under this definition.

The action of a rod is discussed in terms of its speed. A "fast" rod has less flex in its tip and will be somewhat stiffer than a softer or "slow" one. Slow rods are more forgiving of your casting errors, since with a slow rod it will take longer for your rod tip to reach the point where you release the line from your casting hand. This extra margin of time can be particularly important to novice anglers who have not quite gotten down the knack of casting into tight places like overhangs and cut banks. A fast rod, however, offers the experienced angler more power for casting into heavy winds and over long distances. Also, you will find that fast rods allow you to feel the lightest of strikes a little bit better than slow ones. However, you must allow for your own tastes here as with the other criteria used in rod selection.

Spend some time checking out the action of the rods you are considering. Pick one up and gently wiggle the rod so that the tip swings back and forth. Now, compare the way that rod felt with the next one on the rack. Did the tip wiggle more or less readily? If it felt as if it took more effort on your part to get the tip of the second rod you tested to move, then that one is faster than the first. Do not whip the rod around, though, as not only will you fail to learn anything vital about the rod's action, but you may succeed in getting yourself asked to leave the store! If you have any doubt as to the relative speed of one rod over another after a quick test, ask the salesperson.

Length

The second point to take into account is the length of your new ultralight rod. Ultralight rods range from about 4½ feet up to 6 feet in length. Smaller rods are ideal for casting in heavily grown-over areas on small brooks, while longer rods are better used on open rivers and lakes. As in fly-fishing, it is wise to have several rods of different lengths in your quiver.

Here is why.

The first problem an angler faces when fishing on a big piece of water like the ocean or a large lake is the frequent need to make long exploratory casts. Most of the bluefish I have caught were either hooked just beyond the back of a breaking wave or just beyond earshot of a moving boat. Fall short of your mark in either of these situations, and your lure falls harmlessly into the surf's backwash or into a stretch of dead water. Getting enough power behind my cast was key to any success I had.

Logically, then, on big water you want to get as much into each cast as possible to make sure that you will be casting into productive water. A 4½- to 5-foot rod with soft or slow action is less apt to help you here, especially on a large piece of open water where wind can also cause you trouble. You need a long, fast rod that can deliver the kind of punch necessary to put your lure a good distance from you so as to beat the waves or allow you to sneak up to a feeding school of fish without their becoming aware of your presence.

Good selections for long ultralight rods might include Daiwa's Eliminator, which comes in an extra-long 7½-foot length and breaks down into two pieces. The Fenwick Willow rod comes in a 6-foot length and is an excellent alternative.

Short rods have their own special value to the ultralight angler. I do a good deal of fishing for spawning brown and brook trout during the fall in a tiny little brook that runs at the edge of my home property. Each September, after the first major rainstorm of the month, my brook fills up with spawning brook trout. They occupy the upper reaches of the stream. As they begin to spawn, they will work themselves even farther upstream, avoiding the larger brown trout and taking over the tiny nooks of the top water to these streams, which only they

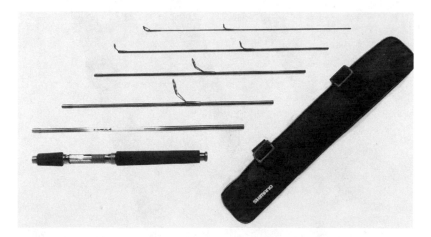

Backpackers and hikers want pack rods when they take to the woods. This one, Shimano's Stimula, breaks down into six pieces and can be strapped onto even the smallest day pack. A pack rod is also excellent for air travel, since it can be brought on board as carry-on luggage and stowed under the seat. (Courtesy Shimano Corporation)

can survive in. Brookies are best able to live in the super-cold headwaters of rivers and brooks, and they will choose these pure, unspoiled habitats to spawn in for the better survival of their young once they hatch next spring.

I go out fishing for these trout the first night after the first big storm after Labor Day, with my smallest ultralight rod and light-

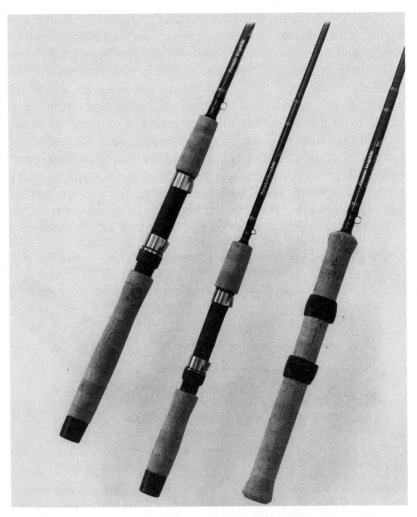

Is the size of the grip suitable to your hand? Do you prefer the feel of imported cork (above) or foam-covered grips? These are important questions to answer. (Courtesy St. Croix Corporation)

est line. The fish I find are extremely aggressive and hit my line almost the instant the lure lands on the water. These spawning trout are very territorial, and far less finicky than usual. They rush toward my oncoming lures and swipe at them angrily. They clearly are not interested in feeding on them, given their attention to mating, but nonetheless they attack in a sideways, slashing motion which indicates that they are highly excited and agitated by the lure's presence.

The trick to this kind of fishing is getting your lure into the right place, and this can be tough when you find yourself fishing on a piece of water that is no more than 10 feet wide and hidden by heavy growth. Also, since my favorite brook has lots of cut banks where brook trout love to hide, flicking my lure between the tree limbs and under the shallow bank without hanging it up can be far more of a challenge than bringing in my fish on the light line I like to use.

A very small rod, say one of only 4½ feet in length, can be extremely valuable during this effort. There are a couple of schools of thought as to whether to use a fast or slow rod in close quarters. Personally, while I prefer a fast rod like the Fenwick Legacy or HMG rod, or even St. Croix's Legend or Premier, for ultralight fishing, I will break out my Daiwa Black Widow, which is somewhat slower than any of these other four rods, when I go after fall-running brookies. I feel I get a bit more bounce in my cast when I attempt to pitch my lure into a cut bank with the slower rod, even though I do sacrifice a little of the sensitivity which the faster rods offer.

The Feel of the Rod

The third thing to consider is the feel of your rod. Most people walk into a tackle shop and either grab the first rod off the rack or confine themselves to testing the flex of each rod by shaking it around, finally selecting the one with the most action and wiggle in the tip. Few will consider that they must spend hours and hours on the water handling that rod, and so some attention must be paid to how it fits in the hand. Is it comfortable? Is the grip suitable to the size of your hand? Do you prefer the feel of foam-covered grips or imported cork? All of these are important questions to consider.

A good friend of mine once told me that he will walk up to a rack of rods, take each one down, one at a time, and just hold it for a few seconds. He says that that is all it takes for him to know whether the grip is right for him. Now, my friend has spent most of the last thirty years as a professional angler, and it will obviously be a lot easier for him to know just what the right feel is for him than it was when he first started out in his career. If you are just starting in ultralight fishing, you might have a little trouble, so here are a few guidelines for you to follow in testing for a rod that suits you.

I find that the best testing ground for new rods is at one of the many fishing expositions that take place around the country each winter (see chapter 2). Using the casting pool at an expo can help you winnow out those rods and reels that do not interest you and let you make your selection from gear that fits your own needs and style of fishing. You can test rods for their action and get hands-on experience with one or several rods before you make a purchase. A good local tackle dealer is also a tremendous resource for information. Remember, his greatest chance of getting you to come back to his store is in giving you accurate information and advice appropriate to your needs. Make use of both expos and tackle shops when looking for your fishing rod.

When looking over the different rods you might find at an expo or tackle shop, start by eliminating all that do not fit your particular style of fishing. For example, if you plan on doing most of your fishing on small mountain streams, you should confine your search to rods under 5 feet in length. If you are shopping for a child, however, try to avoid the temptation to buy a small rod. If that kid is out on the lake with you fishing for walleye or salmon, a 4½-foot rod with 2-pound-test line is going to really frustrate his or her efforts. Choose tackle that is appropriate for the type of water fished on and the species fished for. You will find it much easier to teach a kid how to fish with the right gear than with equipment that is not suited to the task.

Materials

Next, take a look at the material the rod is made from. While there is a certain economical argument for less expensive fiberglass and graphite-composite rods, I urge you to avoid them. The truly best ultralight rods on the market, the ones which will give you the best performance over a long period of time, are the ones made from 100-percent graphite.

Graphite is significantly lighter than fiberglass. While fiberglass does take more abuse than graphite—graphite being a more brittle material—you lose much of the sensitivity that graphite offers an angler. This sensitivity, or "feel," means that you will find it far easier to pick up the vibration of a subtle strike using a graphite rod than with one built out of fiberglass. I have also found that the tip portion of a graphite rod allows you much more power and speed in setting your hook. The shock of a big fish making its run or jumping is more evenly distributed through the entire length of a graphite rod, too, right down to the rod butt.

There is a place for the graphite-composite rod. These rods are made of graphite reinforced with fiberglass fibers for extra strength. They tend to be a little heavier, a bit longer, and less sensitive than 100 percent graphite rods. On the other hand,

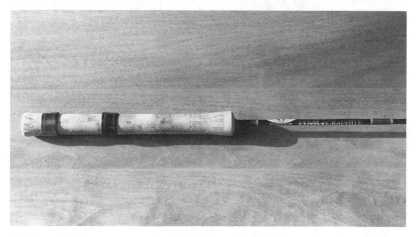

This rod features the famous "Tennessee" style reel seat, similar to those found on fly rods.

they can make very sturdy beginner rods for small children. You see, there is also a fairly impressive price difference between the two materials, with the composite rods costing maybe half what 100 percent graphite rods do.

Matching the Rod to Your Reel

As I emphasized in chapter 2, you must also consider whether your new rod balances with your favorite fishing reel. If you already own a reel, be sure to take it to the tackle shop with you when you go browsing for a rod and strap it onto any rod you consider. If a rod does not balance with your reel, move along to another rod or consider buying another reel to fit your choice—if you are convinced that you have found the fishing rod for you.

I cannot overemphasize the importance of balance. If your reel is too heavy for the rod you have selected, the line will bunch up in the guides as the oversized reel tries to load the rod with more line than your rod is capable of handling. Conversely, if your reel is too small, the line can easily become fouled on the reel itself as your rod tip works to pull off line faster than the reel can release it. You will also find that a poorly balanced rod and reel combo will feel wrong in your hands, and that feeling can become very distracting when you are trying to make delicate or precise casts.

4
The Reels

The motor that keeps your well-oiled fishing rig working right is the reel. For many of us, our choice of which reel to buy is one of the most interesting and confounding we face. While all ultralight reels are designed to do essentially the same thing—namely, retrieve the fishing line we have cast off—there are two important points to ponder before selecting one.

First, consider what species of fish you plan on going after. If you plan on angling for some of the larger fish you are apt to encounter, like northern pike, salmon, or lake trout, you might think about buying one of the heavier-duty reels. Shimano's Symetre 1000 and Stradic 1000 are as good choices as any I can think of, although the Daiwa SS700 Tournament and Daiwa Samuri Long Cast 700 and 705 are also well built for the punishment a big, fast-running fish can exact on your equipment. All of these are somewhat heavier than most ultralight reels, ranging from 7 to almost 9 ounces.

Gear Ratio

The big difference between the heavier Daiwa and Shimano reels here is the gear ratio. While all three Daiwas boast perfectly serviceable 4.4:1 to 4.9:1 ratios, both Shimano reels offer an astonishing 6:1! Abu Garcia also makes a very fine reel called the Cardinal Pro Max which features a 5.4:1 gear ratio. The Abu Garcia reels are extremely compact, which is very desirable, and both weigh about 7½ ounces, making them very powerful packages with which to pursue trophy fish.

Gear ratio is extremely important to consider. A salmon, for instance, will attain speeds of up to 60 miles per hour during its pursuit of your bait and the subsequent fight. When a big fish rushes you, you must be ready to pull in huge amounts of line in an extremely short period of time. On the other hand, it is equally important that your reel be ready to give back that line, either by back-reeling (See "Special Reel Features" below) or with a sufficiently strong drag.

If you plan on going after smaller fish like trout or bass, you can try the tiny Mitchell 600, which weighs only 6.5 ounces. It has a smaller gear ratio too, 4.9:1, which is perfectly ample power for fish up to 4 pounds. Another alternative is the Cardinal Gold Max from Abu Garcia. This reel weighs a little more than the Mitchell, but it is an extremely small package with an impressive 5.4:1 gear ratio.

Another good choice is the Shimano FX-100. This is an inexpensive reel which features a 4.2:1 gear ratio. It only weighs about 7 ounces, and you can spool up to 105 yards of 6-pound line on it. For just a little more money, there is the Shimano AX-100Q, another tiny reel with an affordable price tag. Weighing only 7.4 ounces, it holds the same amount of line as the FX-100. The FX-100 does boast a somewhat more impressive gear ratio of 5.2:1 though, making it an extremely good buy for just under $30. You might also consider Shimano's AX-ULS, at about the same price, which weighs only 5.3 ounces.

While all the reels I've mentioned here will be more than adequate for your needs, there's still one more point you should keep in mind: value. Most of the reels I've discussed cost from $30 to around $100. These are definitely not the bargain basement reels figuring in all those prepackaged fishing combos that fill most mail-order catalogues and tackle shop windows. I purposely have not talked much about these less expensive rigs because I truly believe in the old adage that you get what you pay for. A cheaply built reel may feel good when you pay for it in the store, but where will it leave you after a solid year of hard fishing? Most bargain reels will not stand up to the punishment of even one season, while a more expensive, better-constructed one will bring you years of service. I have three reels which I've used now for three full seasons, putting 25 to 40 days of use on each every year. All three are still in excellent shape, and I figure to get at least three more years' use out of all of them. That's value.

Special Reel Features

There are a number of interesting options which come on ultra-light reels. The most prominent of these is a "quick fire" trigger device found on the bail which allows the angler to grasp his fishing line and flick the bail over for casting, all in one movement of the forefinger. Many anglers I fish with use reels sporting this option, and thcy all rave about the ease of making casts without having to use one hand to hold the line while the other flips the bail. They happen to be right, too—it *is* easier. The one drawback I have found is that your line can become fouled on the trigger system immediately after you begin to retrieve line. When the slack line is suddenly pulled into place by the bail as you start to bring in line, it sometimes jumps a little, causing it to become tangled on the trigger. I should point out, though, that many anglers I know never experience this difficulty. The fact that it has happened to me and to a few other anglers I know is a bit of a puzzlement. I found it to be such a distraction that I eventually removed the trigger system from my quick-fire reels, something that can be done quite easily with a small screwdriver. I now cast my reels the old-fashioned way, with one hand on my line and the other on the bail.

Another option is the rear drag vs. front drag system. This allows anglers to tighten or loosen the drag on their lines either by a dial mounted on top of the spool or by one mounted underneath the bottom. I do not feel there is a big argument in favor of one over the other. However, I have often heard devotees of each system say that they feel theirs allows them better control in adjusting the drag while fighting a fish. I find this a very peculiar attitude. You should always have your drag set properly before you go out on the water so as to maximize the amount of strain your rod and line can take.

In order to do this, I suggest you begin each fishing trip by holding your rod in an upright position, as though you were fighting a fish, and have a friend pull on the end of your line, walking steadily backward away from you. Loosen or tighten the drag until your friend can pull line out without putting so much strain on the rod that it begins to bow by more than a 45-degree angle from where the rod tip was when you held it in the beginning. The reel drag should offer resistance to your friend's pull but allow the line to come off the spool evenly. Your drag will now be set to fight anything from the smallest panfish to the largest northern pike.

High-quality ultralight spinning reels, like this Spirex 500F from Shimano, feature all-aluminum spools. Aluminum combines the advantages of light weight with durability, making for a long-lasting reel and good value. (Courtesy Shimano Corporation)

Of course, some anglers prefer to avoid using the drag altogether and employ a technique called back-reeling instead. In back-reeling, the angler flips a small switch found on almost every ultralight reel made today (usually located on top of the bottom end of the reel) which allows the reel handle to crank in two directions instead of one. When a fish starts to make a run, the angler rotates the reel so as to allow line to leave the spool, and in this way he keeps up with the fish's progress. Back-reeling does three interesting things. It reduces wear and tear on the reel, as no strain is ever exerted on the drag system. Second, because you are using the reel's handle to control how much line is let out, back-reeling lets you take advantage of the reel's gear ratio in governing the speed at which line is let out. Finally, back-reeling puts far less strain on your fishing line, since line does not stretch as much when you manually let it out as it does when the fish pulls line off the reel against the drag.

Materials

Two other choices involve the materials used in making the reel and the number of ball bearings used. The ball bearing issue is an odd one, and one you should be careful of.

Manufacturers are claiming to make reels with anywhere from two to eight ball bearings. Ball bearings make for smoother action on reels, right? Sounds great, doesn't it? Fact is, however, that one of those ball bearings is usually used as the line guide on the bail, and so you begin to see how deceptive these claims can be. While having an extra ball bearing or two related to the rotation of the spool does make for some difference in the performance of a spinning reel, what the reel actually feels like when you are using it is far more important than the number of bearings used to make it. Does the reel rotate smoothly? How quickly does it retrieve line?

You should also be asking questions about the materials used in the making of your new reel. The three basic groups of materials used are cast metal (usually steel), graphite, and aluminum. Most of the less expensive reels are made from either of the first two materials, while the aluminum reels tend to be pricier. Both graphite and aluminum resist corrosion better than the cast-metal reels, and they also tend to be a bit lighter.

I have owned reels made from all three materials and generally prefer the graphite and aluminum construction, favoring the aluminum when asked to choose between the two. I am impressed by how light both kinds of reels are and how well they both stand up to heavy use. The aluminum reels I own also seem to last a little longer than the graphite reels, although I should add that I have had one graphite reel now for ten years and it still performs beautifully for me.

5
The Line

I n this chapter, we are going to take a look at possibly the most underrated piece of equipment used in ultralight fishing—fishing line. In many cases, this is the weak link in the chain of a spinning setup. That's because, while most of us spend an enormous amount of time, money, and effort in selecting our rods and reels, the line we use is often bought as an afterthought. Some folks just figure that the $100–$150 they shell out for the ultralight rod and spinning reel is enough! So, they chintz on the line by grabbing whatever is on special that day. Not that good lines do not end up on sale every once in a while, but I think you should have a few other things in mind than price when it comes to line selection.

Monofilament Lines

It is interesting to note how much fishing line has evolved. In the seventeenth century, when Izaak Walton was writing about fishing, horsehair was a most popular material. Braided lines made from linen, cotton, or silk were utilized later on. All these lines required lengthy drying time between uses to prevent rot. In 1938, Du Pont researchers developed nylon, which was soon adapted to create the first generation of braided synthetic fishing lines. Monofilament lines like the ones we know today were first developed and sold in the United States by Du Pont in 1958 under the trade name, Stren®.

In general, ultralight fishing is confined to lines of 4-pound test or less, although 6- and 8-pound lines are recommended for the larger species like salmon, bluefish, and northern pike. Unfortunately, this simple rule in no way diminishes the confusion you are apt to experience when confronted with the many types of fishing line to choose from. Different lines are designed to do very different things, and you should approach the task of selecting your line carefully, thoughtfully, and with an open mind.

When I first started to fish with ultralight gear, the vast majority of time I had spent fishing with fly gear had been spent on the ocean with my 10-foot surfcasting rod, its large 16-ounce Shimano reel filled with either 12- or 17-pound-test Stren® line. I always chose Stren®, an unusually elastic line, because I found it helped me when fighting my favorite game fish, the bluefish. Blues are famous for their hard strikes, long runs, and high jumps, all of which can cause a lot of stress on a fishing line, not to mention the rest of your gear and your own body.

I began my ultralight career, then, with 4-pound-test spools of the line I knew best. Now, while I still use Stren® a good deal of the time I am out on the water, I also make use of several other lines. In order to determine which line to use on any given day, I go through a simple process.

First, examine what you want to do with that line. If, for example, you figure you will be spending a lot of your time fishing for trout on small, clear-running brooks, you might consider buying one of the several small-diameter lines like Bagley's Silver Thread, Abu Garcia's Ultracast, Fenwick's Liteline, Berkley's Trilene UltraThin, or Stren's Magnathin. To get an idea of how thin these lines really are, consider that 4-pound-test Trilene XL (Extra Limp) has a diameter of .008-inch while Trilene UltraThin will only run to .006-inch in the same weight.

All four of these lines offer you the advantage of being tough for fish to detect. They also are easy to cast, as they offer very little friction on the spool of your reel. That means your casts will be long, and because these light lines encounter much less wind resistance than heavier lines, your casts will tend to run truer as well. This can be especially important when casting in and around heavy overhangs, into small pieces of pocket water, and under cut banks.

Light lines also allow you a bit more sensitivity when fishing for bass with jigs. I have always had a great deal of trouble feeling that tiny *tick* which signals that a bass has mouthed my leadhead jig. It takes an angler of nice judgment and good concentration to discern this faint motion from that of the jig's tumble over a rock or a submerged tree limb. The small-diameter line will give you a bit of an edge here because it does not stretch, a feature which enables the line to transmit somewhat more accurately the vibration of the bass's strike as it moves up the rod to your hands.

The only drawback to light lines is that they may not hold up to the power of a fast-running or hard-hitting fish in large rivers or on lakes as well as a monofilament like Stren® or Berkley's Trilene, which are both designed to take more stress. Both of these lines are designed to stretch when the fish hits, and that stretch allows you a lot more play than you have with a light line. Again, while any monofilament will be compromised by a chance nick, both Stren® and Trilene stand up better than any of the light lines we have discussed. Berkley makes three types of Trilene: XT (Extra Tough), XL (Extra Limp), as well as UltraThin. XT is very strong line which resists abrasion, while XL has very low "line memory." Line memory is the coiling of the line when it is not in use. Limp lines are a fabulous innovation as they do not retain that tight coil which most other lines exhibit after a period of time on your reel, or even on the package spool.

Post-Monofilament Lines

A growing number of ultralight anglers are taking to the water with a post-monofilament generation of lines designed to offer extra protection from the initial shock of a big fish's strike. Prime Plus and Berkley's TriMax both offer the extra strength of being two lines in one—offering the sensitivity characteristic of light lines as well as the extra strength of heavier ones. In the case of Prime Plus, the line is covered with a sheath which can make up roughly a quarter of the line's total volume. TriMax is a blend of polymers which are designed to resist water absorption. Both of these lines resist stretch due to strain or due to the line's becoming waterlogged, a real problem with conventional monofilament lines. Once soaked through, monofilament lines become quite springy and will stretch quickly out of shape, meaning your line could become weakened in one or more spots. Both Prime Plus and TriMax offer the angler a good feel of each strike, extra strength, and longer life on your reel. They are excellent lines with which to fish jigs, crankbaits, and small spinnerbaits, as they will be better able to survive the routine bumps along rocks and logs which go with using these lures.

A very new development in fishing line began to make the rounds in early 1993. Fine-diameter, high-test lines made from braided synthetics were introduced by several companies and have received a good deal of attention due to their great strength and fine feel. Du Pont discovered a high-strength fiber called Kevlar in 1965 which has made its way into high-performance whitewater canoes, bullet-proof vests, and skis, among other applications. Kevlar is five times stronger than steel, pound for pound. Stren® has had a great deal of success with its PowerBraid line, made from Kevlar. AlliedSignal has developed a braided line made from a gel-spun polyethylene called Spectra that is very similar to Kevlar. Berkley, PRADCO, Fenwick, and the Triple Fish Company all have come up with gel-spun polyethylene lines as well. Prices for these new, ultrastrong lines range from $13 to $23 for a 150-yard spool, roughly double what monofilament line costs.

The big advantages to the new braided lines are increased strength from a line with superlight thinness. For example, you should expect a monofilament line with a diameter of .010- to .013-inch to be about 8-pound test, but you can get three to four times that strength from the same diameter Kevlar or other polyethylene braided line. Spectra's new line in 80-pound test is only .015-inch in diameter. There are a few disadvantages, though. The new braided lines are actually so strong that they have been known to score some makes of inexpensive rod guides. Also, most manufacturers today seem to be interested in making high-test lines for tournament and big game fishing. It may be a little while before we see many examples of this type of line in ultra-light weights, although Stren® and Fenwick are making 6- and 8-pound lines in this material now.

Line Colors

Another thing to consider is the color of your line. Lines come in fluorescent colors, camouflage, and ultraclear. Personally, I prefer the clear lines, even though there is evidence showing that colored lines can be extremely effective in certain circumstances. I feel that your line should be as invisible as possible so that the fish keys in on your lure, and this is why I figure clear line is your best choice for most angling situations. This preference goes back to my training as a fly-angler. The object of fishing with artificials is to trick the fish by sight or vibration, I was always told. Anything that inhibited that effort was to be avoided.

Having said this, I should explain some of the rationale behind the coloring of fishing line. Fluorescent lines are often

Line diameter is very important. A light line will seem almost invisible to fish on a bright day, but a heavier line can be necessary if you are fishing for large species along a rocky lake bottom. (Courtesy Stren)

recommended by anglers who feel most comfortable checking for subtle strikes by sight. Many bass anglers like to fish their jigs and crankbaits this way and must be able to watch the line when they allow their bait to free-fall. Fluorescent lines also show up very well at night if you shine an ultraviolet light on them. Moss-colored or camouflaged lines are most often used by anglers working water that has an overabundance of algae in it. Again, many of these anglers are bass specialists and do their fishing during the heat of midsummer. The idea is that these tinted lines will blend into the murk of the stained water, becoming essentially invisible to the fish.

Changing Line

A couple of other thoughts on fishing line: How often should you change your line? Line can become twisted or even nicked by normal casting and stretching when you are out on the water. It therefore makes sense to change it after every 12 to 24 hours of use. This means that if you spend a full day pounding the water on your favorite stream, you should respool the next day. If you only have time to hit the water after work for a couple of hours at a time, you can let things slide for a half-dozen of those shorter trips before putting fresh line on your reel.

Another good reason for changing your line often has to do with line memory. As has already been explained, line will conform to the pattern of the coils it wraps itself into when it is left on a reel spool for long periods of time. This in turn causes the line to snag when you cast it, as it will not unspool properly. By changing your line regularly, you avoid this pitfall entirely.

Some anglers also like to straighten their newly purchased line, right out of the packaging spool. One way of doing this is to fill the reel with the line and then have a friend hold onto the free end. Open up your reel bail and back away from your friend a good 50 or 60 yards. Have your friend let go of his end. Run the line between the thumb and forefinger of the hand that holds your rod as you reel it in. In this way, you will be using your fingers to untwist the length of line that you and your friend pulled out, eliminating kinks and snarls.

If you do not already own a spare spool for your favorite reel, you should consider buying one and filling it with fresh line to hold in reserve. Some experienced anglers will even put a light line on one spool and a heavier-duty monofilament on the other so that they can better adapt to changing water conditions.

Whether you are at home or on the water, dispose properly of any line you discard. Many line manufacturers—Berkley, for instance—sponsor line recycling programs. Aside from the obvious fact that improperly disposed-of line is litter and is therefore unpleasant, there are a couple of other reasons for care that you might want to keep in mind. First, monofilament and copolymer lines take next to forever to decompose in the environment. The Cornell University Cooperative Extension Service reports that while it takes regular nylon fabric 30 to 40 years to break down and glass bottles close to a million years, fishing line can stay intact almost indefinitely. Second, since line

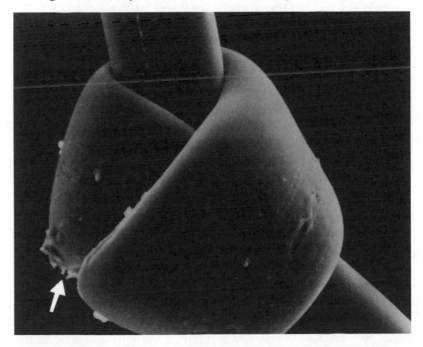

If a chain is only as strong as its weakest link, then fishing line is the link you should examine carefully for wear and tear before you go out on the water. (Courtesy Stren)

THE IMPROVED CLINCH KNOT

Knots are important, as an inappropriate or badly tied knot can unnecessarily weaken your line. I use one knot for about 90 percent of all fishing situations. The improved clinch knot will hold your line to lures and swivels (when you are using downriggers) and can even be used to attach two pieces of line to each other.

1. Put the end of the line though the eye of the lure or swivel. Double it back and wind it around the standing length of line five times. Thread the end of the line through the small loop above the eye and then through the larger loop you have just created.

2. Hold the end of the line while you pull on the lure or swivel, causing the coils in the standing length of line to pull up. Be sure the coils are spiraled as shown in the drawing and are tight against the eye. Trim excess line.

does not break down, it can really wreak havoc with bird life. Birds are easily ensnared by line that has blown into tree branches. Your high-tech monofilament can be a killer or a maimer of these unwitting creatures.

Finally, I recommend that you not use snap swivels. These little devices were designed to prevent your line from twisting around itself as your lure moves through the water. They work: twisted line does weaken, and indeed the swivel minimizes this. Snap swivels also allow you to change your lure a little more quickly than you can if you tie a new one on every time you change. On the other hand, swivels, like steel leaders (also designed to save your line by placing a strong buffer between it

JOINING TWO LENGTHS OF LINE

1. **Overlap the ends of two lengths of fishing line by about six inches. Take one end and twist it around the other line once, leaving a loop.**

2. **Then twist the looped piece of line around the other line five times, finally passing the end through the loop you made.**

3. **Tighten the knot.**

4. **Repeat the procedure with the remaining length of line. You will be left with two clinch knots, separated by a few inches.**

5. **Pull on the two pieces of line simultaneously. This will bring the two clinch knots together, binding the two pieces of line. Trim the ends.**

and the sharp teeth of fish like salmon, pike, or bluefish) are easily detectable by a fish's keen eyesight. In clear water or on sunny days, a fish's eyes can see even better than usual, and anything that does not look completely natural can get in the way of your success. My advice is that you leave your steel leaders at home and only bring out the swivels when you use a downrigger. I will have more to say on that subject in chapter 11.

6
The Lures

There are so many lures on the market: lures designed to float on the surface, lures meant to dive to great depths, lures with lots of flash and wiggle, and lures tooled to make noise and generate flutter. There are also a whole lot of lures out there that have been built with the idea of catching fishermen rather than fish. Remember, no fish ever bought a fishing lure; it's anglers like you and me who often end up buying lures because they "look right," or they have a "real nice action."

I have a theory that while many people I know make very good anglers, many of the anglers I know would make lousy fish. They would only strike at those lures I mentioned that "look right" or have a "nice action." Frankly, the lures that we're certain are just right may not be at all what a fish will even consider.

Let me give you one of my favorite examples of a lure designed to catch people rather than fish. About twenty years ago, my dear mother decided to give me something really unique as a Christmas present. She knew I already had a good collection of lures that I used to catch bluefish and striped bass on the ocean and smallmouth bass and perch on the lakes I used to frequent. My favorites were almost exclusively spoons, although I was also known to toss an occasional top water lure when the action slowed down on those windless days in the middle of the summer. My mother, the genius of our family for locating strange and exotic little gifts as stocking stuffers, went on a quest to find the damnedest lure she could lay her hands on.

I will never know exactly how exhaustive her search for that lure was. What I do know is that on that fateful Christmas morning, she smiled triumphantly as I opened her gift, a tiny hollowed-out plastic replica of a fish in an equally tiny box that proclaimed this lure to be, "The World's Only Self-Propelled Fishing Lure!"

The secret to this amazing advance in angling technology was that you could unscrew the lure, revealing a special cavity which you were supposed to fill with soda pellets that were enclosed in the same package. Once the water seeped into the lure after your cast, the soda pellets would begin to fizz, theoretically causing the lure to "swim" in an erratic manner as the bubbles released by the dissolving soda pushed it about. What the manufacturer had failed to mention was that the pellets had an extremely short life in the water, and often the swimming effect only lasted a few seconds. Then the lure would react like any other water-filled object and sink unceremoniously to the bottom.

This is a classic case of a marketing ploy designed to make sales but not necessarily to make anglers happy once they go out on the water. I have come across lots of other equally slick but useless inventions over the years, but "The World's Only Self-Propelled Fishing Lure!" has to be my favorite.

So the first order of business when looking at all the lures available to you in tackle shops, catalogues, and department stores is to be a little disbelieving of the claims that the manufacturers make about their products. Remember, there are plenty of ways to get good information on fishing lures and other pieces of fishing equipment. Also keep in mind that you really should only be interested in lures that weigh less than ¼ ounce, as these will be the most applicable for ultralight gear.

The best thing to do is to consult friends of yours who have used a lure that you are thinking of buying. How did it work? Under what conditions did it perform best? Was it most useful when water temperatures were warm or cool? Did it catch the species of fish you want to catch? Did the lure require any type of modification or adjustment when used? Did it catch more fish on cloudy days or on days when the sun was out? You should also ask specifically where your friends used the lure. Was it successful on water where you normally fish? If not, where did they find the lure worked best? If you are fishing in waters you are not familiar with and you do not know anyone who has fished there, ask a local tackle shop owner his opinion. Tackle salespeople who take their work seriously want you to succeed with the lures they sell you. It is the one sure way they can get you to come back and to recommend them to your friends. With these thoughts in mind, let us look at some of the lures you will find on the market shelves.

Spoons

The earliest spoon lures were actually made out of old tableware. The bowl of a spoon was often used, as was a knife handle and its blade, to make three very different kinds of lure. The spoon bowl, being concave, would be attached to a wire which was also fastened to a hook. The bowl would flutter madly in the water as the contraption was retrieved, much the way the modern spinnerbait and the spinner are used. I will discuss these two types of lures later, but it is important to remember that all three lures—the spoon, the spinnerbait, and the spinner—are related in this way.

The lures made from the blade and handle of a knife were far more like the spoon lures we are familiar with today. The blade of a butter knife was often bent or hammered so that its irregular shape would cause it to flutter and flash underwater. Holes were drilled at either end of the blade, one for tying the fishing line and the other for attaching hooks. The handle was often drilled in the same way and then hammered so as to dimple the handle's surface with indentations that would catch the sun's rays and cause the lure to flash. Fork handles were also used from time to time, as they were usually already bent and would snake their way through the water when retrieved.

Understand that a standard cutlery lure kit is rarely suitable for the kind of ultralight angling you plan on doing. However, the basic principle of a long, flat metal object which has been doctored to enhance flutter or flash is still central to the design of spoon lures.

Some of the more popular spoon lures available are Acme's Kastmaster, the Phoebe, and the Little Cleo. These lures have been around since the 1940s and are meant to imitate the flash of a wounded minnow. They all feature smooth surfaces and rely on flutter to attract fish. The Hopkins lure is a hammered spoon which, while it does flutter some in the water, uses the dozens of hammered facets along its sides to catch and reflect light. The famous Johnson Silver Minnow is a concave lure with a single hook that is welded to the inner curve. It wobbles and darts wildly through the water and is often equipped with a thin metal wire which prevents it from hanging up on weeds. The Mooselook Wobbler is another curved spoon which vaguely resembles a fish. This is one of the most potent salmon lures on the market and is in very high demand.

There are dozens and dozens of other variations like the Dardevle, the Rebel Arrowhead, and the Red Eye, as well as Luhr Jenson's Super Duper and Krocodile. All are designed on the same basic premise, that light and movement will attract fish. Also, you should know that no spoon lure will work at depths of greater than a couple of feet unless you are using a deep-running downrigger.

Spinners and Spinnerbaits

As I mentioned, these types of lures are derivatives of the basic spoon lure. In both cases they are treble hooks attached to a wire that has a small spoon-shaped blade coupled to it. The major difference is that while a spinner has the blade located right at the top of a short, straight piece of wire, the spinnerbait has a blade attached to one end of a piece of wire that has been bent at a right angle. At the other end of the spinnerbait, a weighted hook fixed with either a plastic skirt, a plastic grub, or both, is attached. Both these types of lures rely on the flash and vibration provided by the blade as it rotates around the wire holding it. Spinners are normally buzzed along the top foot or so of the water and attract fish from the depths with all the light and noise they produce. Spinnerbaits can also be brought in along the top, but more often than not they are fished along the contour of a lake or river bottom, much the same way a jig is used (see section on jigs in this chapter as well as chapter 10, "Bass").

The spinner is a simple device and has been used for decades throughout Europe and North America. One of the oldest lines of these lures is the Mepps, which is manufactured in France. The Mepps is the standard by which all spinners have been measured, although some American firms have added interesting variations to this time-tested design. The best known of these is the Rooster Tail, a spinner made by the Yakima Bait Company. This lure has been on the market for almost forty years and was originally made by the Worden Company. Yakima and Worden have merged, and the fine spinning lure they manufacture under their joint names is a very popular one among trout, bass, and salmon anglers. The Panther Martin, the Blue Fox Vibrax, and the Blue Fox Super Vibrax are also well-made spinners and are worth your consideration.

Many spinners feature bucktails, although some, like the Mepps, also have rubber minnows impaled on the treble hooks they trail. Mepps has also come out with a line of single-hook spinners which I like a lot. Not only can they be tipped with plastic grubs, plastic worms, or pork rind, but a single hook makes for far less fuss and fumbling than does a treble when it comes time to release your fish.

Lots of companies make spinnerbaits. Berkley's Power Spin-N-Jig, the Blue Fox Black Flash, and Stanley's Wedge are all excellent examples of what a spinnerbait should be. All three of these lures feature a sturdy wire frame, high-flash blades, brightly colored skirts, and large single hooks. The Black Flash has an extra modification, a black frame, which adds to the illusion that the blade and hook head are separate, to simulate schooling baitfish. The main difference between these spinnerbaits is the shape of the blades. Blades come in a dazzling array of colors, sizes, and shapes. For that matter, there is an equally remarkable selection of skirt colors available.

Many anglers I know have started to make their own spinnerbaits, combining skirts made from Spandex, rubber, and silicone with nickel, copper, and brass blades. Many even make their own bait frames and leadhead sinkers to attach to the hooks with mold kits. Lead ingots, lead melters, molds, straight spring-tempered wire, and wire-forming tools are available from tackle shops and catalogues all over the country.

In regard to selecting the colors you will want to use in choosing or making your lures, consult friends who have fished

The Rooster Tail is one of the best-known spinning lures available. This model, the Rooster Tail Lite, is specifically made for ultralight fishing. (Courtesy Yakima Bait Company)

the waters you will be using the lures on. Remember, firsthand knowledge is invaluable in avoiding lures that are designed merely to catch anglers instead of fish!

Crankbaits

Most good crankbaits are made of balsa wood and are carved to look like a minnow. They range in size from just a couple of inches to 9 inches long and feature two sets of treble hooks that dangle below the lure. Affixed to the lure's nose is a lip which can vary in length from less than ½ inch to over 2 inches. The lip length is what regulates the depth a crankbait will dive to; the longer the lip the deeper the dive. While most of the crankbaits I have used float on the water immediately after hitting the surface, there also are sinking ones which you can allow to settle to a desired depth before retrieving. Floating crankbaits can also be used for top water fishing as surface plugs.

The classic crankbait came from Finland and from the fertile mind of a man named Lauri Rapala. An American, Ronald Weber, met Rapala in 1962, and the two soon began manufacturing Rapala's invention, a balsa wood lure that was designed to dive to a cruising level as it was retrieved. This lure was called the CountDown and was hailed as a major innovation in

This crankbait is designed for deep diving. Note the long lip on the lure's nose. (Courtesy Bagley Bait Company)

angling tackle. Since this time, many other manufacturers have gotten into the market, and there is now a mind-boggling array of floating and sinking crankbaits to choose from.

While the Rapala crankbait is in many ways still the industry standard, other innovators have introduced crankbaits that deserve some discussion. The Yakima Bait Company has developed a fabulous lure called the Flatfish. This crankbait is a little different from the standard long-billed lure. The bill is actually an extension of the main body, which dips down, creating a sharp bend along the front line of the bait. The line is tied up an inch or more above the tip of the nose so that the dip in the nose causes the lure to dive when it is retrieved.

Bagley also makes a couple of fine crankbaits, the Bitty-B and the Bang-O. Rebel is famous for its light-line baits, the Wee Frog, the Cat'R Crawler, and of course their impressive line of Minnows and Spoonbill Minnows. The world-famous Zara line from Heddon is also a very good bet.

Most good crankbaits are made of balsa wood and are carved to look like a minnow. They feature two sets of treble hooks that dangle below the lure. This Bagley's Bang-O lure is a good example of a well-made crankbait.

Finally, we should take a quick look at the variety of crankbaits known as Rattlers. The Bill Lewis Lure Company makes what they call the Original Rat-L Trap, a diamond-shaped, hollow metal lure that is filled with small pieces of lead shot. When this diving bait is retrieved, the lure shakes and vibrates, causing the shot to rattle around inside. This action makes a lot of noise underwater and is known to attract fish from quite a long way off. In fact, if you sit in your boat or canoe very quietly as you bring one of these lures in, you can hear the rattling sound from a good distance. Rattling lures are also made by Rapala, Cotton Cordell, Storm, Mann's, and Bill Norman.

Jigs and Plastic Worms

As fishing lures go, there is nothing more basic than a jig. It is a hook that has been embedded in a lead head, commonly weighing either ⅛ or ¼ ounce, although smaller lead heads in $\frac{1}{12}$- and $\frac{1}{16}$-ounce sizes are also available. The lead head is sometimes painted and may even feature an oversized set of eyes. The hook is dressed either with feathers, a piece of pork rind, or a plastic grub. The classic plastic worm is sewed onto a hook so that the hook barb ends up embedded in the body of the worm and is weighted down with a small lead head that is attached to the top of the worm head or slid up a foot or so on the line itself.

These lures are almost always fished along the bottom and are extremely effective on small- and largemouth bass. You bounce your jig along at a very slow speed and wait for the tell-tale *tick* on your line that signals that a fish has taken your lure. The fact that you will be fishing in rocky terrain, often filled with submerged logs and other debris, guarantees that you will lose a good number of your jigs and worms. There really is not a great deal you can do about this, and you should consider it part of the price of fishing with these types of lures. Fortunately, both are inexpensive to buy and even cheaper to make yourself. As with the spinnerbait, jig-making kits are readily available. If after reading the chapter in this book on bass you find that fishing with jigs appeals to you, I strongly urge you to consider buy-ing a kit and making your own jigs at home. It is a lot of fun and will save you quite a bit of money in the long run.

7

Gadgets and Gizmos

T he contents of your tackle box often will reveal more about your personality than even the most sophisticated and scientific psychological analysis. What an angler picks in the way of accessories to complement his or her selection of lures, rods, and reels tells much about the angler, his aspirations, and his habits on the water. While I feel that the contents of an angler's tackle box are very personal and therefore should not be judged by others, I also think there are some gadgets that really do belong in every ultralight angler's box. These are a few items that I have found indispensable when it comes to ultralight fishing.

Knife

A good knife is absolutely the number one, most important piece of equipment to pack along. The Swiss Army style of knife is perhaps the best because so many useful accessories are tucked away inside it. Some of these multipurpose knives carry just a few too many options, however, so I would like to give you a checklist of things to look for in your knife.

Obviously, you will want a good-sized blade. The main blade of your knife should be strong enough to cut half-inch-diameter rope with ease and also be sharp enough to gut a freshly caught fish. I am not sure it is necessary for you to be able to fillet a fish with your knife, though, as this is a task that can easily be done at home after you have finished fishing. (Also, some states require that the whole fish carcass be kept intact until you return home, to facilitate field inspection by game wardens.) You should be able to scale most fish, even with a small blade of only 3 inches.

A pair of scissors is also very useful, especially for trimming line, fly hackle from streamers, and plastic spinnerbait skirts, and for snipping your line to release fish with hooks too deeply embedded in their jaws to remove safely.

A bottle opener is an absolute must, as is a can opener. Lunch out on the water is simply impossible without them.

Phillips and flathead screwdrivers are extremely important options. I have found that on the water repairs to reels are next to impossible with only a knife blade. Be sure your knife has both types of screwdriver heads on it.

A good knife is absolutely the most important piece of equipment to pack. The Swiss Army style of knife is perhaps the best because so many useful accessories are tucked away in it. (Courtesy Buck Knives Inc.)

Surgical Forceps

A small pair of forceps is your best answer to the question of how to quickly and safely release most fish. Forceps allow you to get a much better hold of the hook with one hand while your other hand keeps the fish steady. Long-nosed forceps will allow you to reach deeper into a fish's mouth to retrieve hooks that have been inhaled down into the back of the fish's throat. Remember, though, if you see blood coming out of the gill area, the overwhelming odds are that your fish is fatally wounded and cannot be released. Like the standard forceps, but a bit more useful with larger species like bluefish, barracuda, and northern pike, is a device called a Hook Out. The Hook Out has a 7-inch-long stainless steel shaft, on a trigger handle, that leads to a small pair of pincers. This device allows you to reach down deep into the jaws of a large, toothy fish to remove lures without risking your fingers in the process. Both the Hook Out and forceps are vital to safe fishing.

If you run across some truly big fish like 40-inch 'cudas or 20-pound blues or stripers, you will also probably want a good heavy set of stainless steel pliers. Bluefish in particular can be

A small pair of forceps is your best answer to the question of how to release most fish quickly and safely.

very hard to release as they have large, bony jaws. Hooks caught in these jaws can be very tough to remove without the extra strength a good set of pliers offers.

I would like to point out that forceps, Hook Outs, and pliers are not the best tools for removing hooks deeply embedded in *you*. Hooks that slip and bury themselves past the point where the barb can be seen are very dangerous. You can be in real trouble if you hook yourself severely when out in the wild. The best way to remove a hook that has sunk into your flesh is to take about 3 feet of fishing line and fold it either in half or quarters so that you have made two or four strands out of the original length. Insert the strands so that they touch the concave side of the hook and are lightly straining against the hook shaft. Quickly and cleanly, pull the line back along the route by which the hook entered your body. Surprisingly, you should feel almost nothing as the hook pops free! You should always wash out the wound as soon as possible to prevent infection.

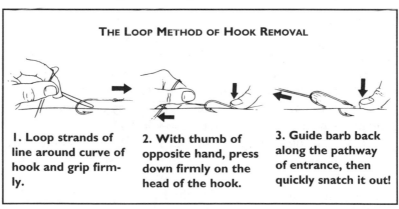

THE LOOP METHOD OF HOOK REMOVAL

1. Loop strands of line around curve of hook and grip firmly.

2. With thumb of opposite hand, press down firmly on the head of the hook.

3. Guide barb back along the pathway of entrance, then quickly snatch it out!

Thermometer

Throughout this book, you will read that certain fish are best pursued in water that is in a specific range of temperature. It therefore makes sense to be able to test the water for its temperature when you go fishing. A thermometer can give you some idea as to whether fish are going to be in a frenzy of activity or whether you are going to have to work a little harder to catch them.

There are lots of thermometers out on the market, and most of them will suit your purposes just fine. Some, like the model sold by Bass Pro, also offer you a depth gauge so that you can sample temperatures from various depths. It does not really make much difference what kind of thermometer you choose; just be sure it is small, lightweight and easy to read.

Penlight

Fishing at dusk or even at night is made much simpler with a small pocket flashlight. One of the more inventive pocket-sized designs comes from Streamlight. This light has a special handle that unlatches, allowing you to wrap the two halves around your head. This gives you the convenience of hands-free light for tying on lures, unhooking fish, and making minor repairs in the dark.

Weights and Measures

From the point of view of many anglers, nothing is as important as the stories to be told after the fishing trip is over. Tales of great fish, heroic battles, and the embellishments that make a story fun are at least half the enjoyment of any day on the water. But what good is a great story without the vital statistics? Make sure your stories carry the weight of authenticity by bringing along a scale and a measuring tape each time you go out.

I always bring along both so that I can get a handle on the size of some of the larger fish I catch. My personal best for the various species I go after is a list I treasure. My 22-inch, 5-pound rainbow; the 34-inch, 16-pound bluefish; and the 20-inch, 3¾-pound brown trout I have caught are important milestones in my life. I want to remember them all, and the accurate knowledge of their sizes and weights is what keeps those experiences alive for me every day.

Just about any hardware store can sell you a perfectly adequate measuring tape, but you will have to hit a tackle shop or a catalogue for a good fish scale. Zebco's Fisherman's De Liar is a favorite, as is Cardoza's Peak Reading scale. Both of these scales use a simple spring-operated mechanism and an easy-to-read indicator. Normark makes an electronic digital scale featuring a half-inch-high numerical display that is very useful if you want photo proof of the monster catch of the day.

Hook Sharpener

I really can't tell you just how many fish are lost each year because the hook set was flawed due to a dull point. Millions, I imagine. It therefore makes particular sense to minimize this problem when you are out fishing with the very lightest-weight fishing gear available.

Berkley makes two sharpeners, one selling for under $20 and running on two C batteries. All you have to do is insert the point of the hook into the nose of the sharpener, and the sharpener does the rest. A deluxe model runs on D batteries and uses a slightly larger rotary carbon steel file to hone hooks to a razor point. It sells for just under $25.

Of course, the traditional Hook Honer from Bass Pro, a variation of the old-style sharpening stone, works well too and sells for under $5.

Sun Block

The incidence of skin cancer is growing at an alarming rate. When you are outdoors, it makes good sense to cover up as much as you can. Wear a baseball cap and dark glasses to protect the top of your head and your eyes, and put on a sun block with a sun-protection formula of at least 15 on all exposed skin.

There are also a few items that do not exactly fit into your tackle box, but are well worth bringing along.

Polarized Glasses

In much of fishing, you can't catch what you can't see. Fish do not like bright light, which is why the best times to fish are in the morning and in the evening when the sun is at its lowest. The sun also casts your shadow on the water, which can cause a fish to spook when it sees the shadow move. But by far the greatest problem that faces us when fishing on a sunny day is the glare off the water. It is awfully hard to keep your eyes on a small lure moving at a foot or so down when the sunlight bounces off the water and into your face. Polarized sunglasses can effectively eliminate much of the glare you encounter. There are two basic kinds of polarized lenses, and you should check both of them out before buying. The first are the gray lenses, which offer you relief from glare during the middle portion of the day when the sun is at its highest. The one drawback to the gray lens is that it can become tough to see through as the light begins to dwindle at the end of the day. Yellow polarized lenses are a perfect alternative in this case, as they let more light into your field of view while still filtering out most of the glare.

No matter what kind of glasses you eventually purchase, make sure they are designed to protect your eyes from ultraviolet rays. UV rays can cause great damage to your eyes through prolonged exposure and can literally fry your retinas.

Vest

Most fly-anglers I know wear a multipocketed fishing vest instead of carrying a tackle box. Vests are very convenient, especially if you plan on hiking a good distance while you fish. Vests come with literally dozens of pockets—the one I use now has twenty-eight! There are places for just about everything you need to bring along, including lures, your knife, weights, extra spools of line, etc.

I have owned only two fishing vests over the past twenty-five years. One was an Orvis and the other came from Cabela. Both vests are still completely intact and quite usable. In selecting my vests, I looked for high-quality construction, good stitchwork, and lightweight material.

I also made sure that my vests were tan in color as opposed to the dark camouflage that has become so popular recently. Tan blends in very nicely with your natural surroundings, and unlike dark green camo patterns, tan does not absorb the sun's heat on midsummer days.

Tackle Pack

Skiers have been using the famous "fanny pack" for decades to schlepp along lunch, extra glasses, ski wax, and other items. Recently anglers have begun to use modified versions of these miniature packs with great success. Patagonia makes a pack that can be fastened around your waist or on your chest and holds just about everything an ultralight angler could ever need for a day trip.

Tackle packs are available in a wide assortment of sizes, from the traditional fanny pack all the way up to a downsized backpack. Prices do vary, anywhere from about $50 up to well over $100. Other tackle pack manufacturers include Creek Co. and D. B. Dun.

Net

I am not a big one for carrying nets. This usually means that I have a hell of a time whenever I hook into a really good fish. I fish a lot with a good friend of mine who is never without his net, though, and I always end up hollering for him to come give me a hand when I get into trouble. John is a very patient man, and he seems not to be terribly bothered by my behavior. However, I think I will start carrying a net when I go fishing with him. There are simply too many times when a net is the only safe way to boat or land a fish. If you don't believe me, just check out the chapter on walleyes and northern pike.

Your net should be appropriate to the size of the species you are pursuing. In other words, do not go after an 8-pound walleye with a 2-foot-long trout net. You are liable to find yourself in a mismatch, and the fish will surely win. While there are lots of good nets out there, here are a few quick tips on what to look for.

Only buy nets that are well constructed. Avoid ones made from cheap plastics or inferior grades of aluminum. These nets will not last long and may even bend under the weight of larger fish.

Try to avoid fine nylon netting. While these nets will be very lightweight, which is a big advantage, the fine nylon can cut into fish like trout which have little or no scale protection.

Generally speaking, the fewer moving parts, the better. There are lots of collapsing nets on the market today. Each of them features steel springs that will wear out long before the netting or handle will.

Finally, keep it simple. There are nets equipped with gaff holders, built-in scales, etc. Remember, a net is supposed to help you catch fish! Accessories are not necessary and are really a diversion.

Depth Finder

For the high-tech angler out for a day of trolling, the depth finder is an absolute necessity. In order to keep on top of the changing underwater topography, you have to have accurate, up-to-the-minute information. A good depth finder can offer you this—and sometimes much more.

The most basic depth finder is a dial with a flashing light that tells you the depth of the water you are passing over. A transducer mounted under the transom of the boat bounces sound waves off the bottom to register distance to the lake bottom and any submerged structure.

As you go up the technological ladder, you can buy depth finders that tell you a lot more about the water you're fishing than its depth. There is a whole line of fish-finding sonar devices made by companies like Humminbird, Eagle, Genetron, and Bottom Line that offer liquid crystal display readouts giving an actual picture of the lake bottom. Many also will allow you to print out a graph of the lake bottom for future reference. The fabulous Humminbird Dimension 3 Sonar 600 is equipped to provide you with a three-dimensional rendering of the bottom, complete with detailed blips showing you exactly where fish are holding. This model sells for about $475. The Genetron GT-9 offers full video picture, alarms that are set off when fish are encountered, depth alarms, depth readings to an astonishing 1,500 feet, and lots of other options. It also sells for over $1,500!

For the more frugal angler, there are plenty of options, and you should take a good look at everything, ask lots of questions, and read up on these products before making your purchase.

There are a number of very well built depth finders for sale for $150–$350 that should serve you well.

Finally, we have a gadget that you really cannot bring along with you when you hit the water. However, you should consider owning one and making use of it in between fishing trips or during the off-season.

Lure-Making Kit

A great way to cut your costs when fishing with jigs or spinnerbaits is to make them yourself. Since you fish both these lures along the bottom for bass and other species, you are apt to snag them on rocks, logs, submerged treetops, and other debris. To cut down the expense of lost lures, lots of folks are getting into lure making, and it really can be a lot of fun.

Hilts makes all manner of kits for the angler who wants to get into this hobby. One of the more popular kits is called the Worm Factory. Molds for grubs and worms as well as a good supply of liquid plastic come with this outfit. If your taste runs to poppers or floating baits, there is a Lure Foam Factory, also by Hilts, which gives you everything you need to make your own top water lures.

The biggest craze now is in jig and spinnerbait making. Molds to make ⅛- to ½-ounce lead heads in several shapes are available, as are molds to help you attach straightened wire for your spinnerbait rigs. There are even molds to make those handy plastic worm sinkers.

While Hilts makes kits for all these needs, you should check around for what other manufacturers have to offer. Catalogues like Bass Pro are a good place to start, but do not overlook your local tackle dealer. He may have the same products, and you won't have to pay him a shipping charge.

8
Casting

Your ultralight rod and reel are far more sensitive than any other spinning rig you own. This sensitivity works in two ways: when you cast and when you feel the fish strike. In this chapter, we will concentrate on the former and discuss the various ways you can best make use of your ultralight equipment in casting.

There are four basic casts in spin-fishing: the overhand, the sidearm, the backhand, and the flip.

Overhand and Sidearm

The overhand and sidearm casts are best discussed together, as they are more alike than the other two. In fact, if you examine what they are and how they work, you will find that both the overhand and sidearm casts have a great deal in common with pitching in baseball.

I have always held that baseball and fishing are uniquely intertwined. Both of these sports begin in the spring, normally during the very first days of April, and continue without regard to the heat and humidity of midsummer right until the very end of fall. Both have "second seasons." In baseball it is the World

Series, while for anglers the second season takes place during the dramatic fall spawning runs of salmon and trout. And both sports rely upon the finesse of fine pitching—or, in fishing, casting.

The baseball pitcher approaches his art with a mix of power, grace, and intelligence. He must decide (with his catcher) which pitch, delivered with what velocity, will be most effective against the batter at hand. Similarly, the angler must gauge his opponent, the fish, and deduce precisely which type of cast will be most efficient in landing his lure where it can be best brought back through the water toward his quarry.

In baseball, there are two distinct styles of pitcher, the overhand and the sidearm. My ideal of the most beautiful practitioner of the overhand pitch was always Tom Seaver. He would kick his left foot up high into the air and then, as it fell, his body would begin to tilt toward home plate. As the left foot began to plant itself on the front of the mound, Seaver's right hand, which

The Overhand Cast

had been almost left behind by the forward motion, would begin to rotate upward, the ball squeezed in his fingers. As the weight of his body shifted fully onto his left leg, the right hand would be fully overhead, and it would be only a split second before Seaver would release the ball and let the arm start to swing down as it followed through the pitch.

The sidearm pitcher, on the other hand, reaches back with his pitching arm, kicks the opposite leg, and then swings the hand holding the ball around the outside of his body, carrying it between his shoulder and his waist. The ball is released just after it has passed the pitcher's body, and the follow-through swings across the body.

Although overhand and sidearm casting resemble pitching in many ways, however, there is an important difference. Some pitchers throw overhand, some sidearm. By contrast, overhand and sidearm casting are two tools used for distinctly different situations by the same anglers. I would never recommend that

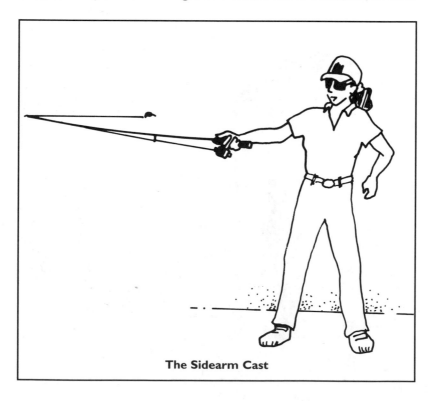

The Sidearm Cast

an angler become exclusively an overhand or sidearm stylist. These types of cast are designed to do different things, and to rely too much on one or the other will greatly limit your effectiveness.

The overhand cast is ideal for placing your lure at a fairly distant spot where pinpoint accuracy is not vital. It is quite possible to put your overhand cast within a foot or so of a target at, say, 40 or 50 feet out. But as you increase the distance, you will end up having to sacrifice some of that accuracy for range. On the other hand, the overhand cast becomes very tough to manage when dealing with distances of less than 40 feet. Here, the overhand approach will tend to overpower, and you will find it almost impossible to hit your target. The sidearm cast is great for shorter situations like this, however, as you can be far more delicate in your touch while casting sidearm and therefore can exert more control over the release of your line.

Let us examine what makes the overhand distinct from the sidearm cast. The overhand cast is made by bringing the tip of your rod directly overhead and releasing the line when the rod

If your feet, shoulders, and hands are all in line with each other and you release your cast at the top of its arc, your lure will follow the path you have chosen.

The Backhand Cast

tip has passed over the top of your head, while the sidearm cast is snapped from approximately a waist-high position and the line is released once the rod tip has come around the side of your body. The overhand cast allows the angler the advantage of power because the entire body, from the arms through the chest and even the legs, can be utilized to generate momentum. The sidearm cast will allow you to zip your line under overhangs or to cast across strong wind currents where it might be advantageous to keep your lure's line of flight low by using only the flicking motion of your arm and wrist.

The overhand cast will always follow a straight line of flight, providing you release it at the top of its arc. In this way, you will be able to take maximum advantage of the momentum you have set up while controlling the direction of the cast. The sidearm cast can also be made to follow a straight line of flight, if you release the line before the rod tip has actually swung past you. In both the sidearm and the overhand cast, you must release your line while the rod tip is in line with your body. The top of the sidearm cast's arc is actually in the same position relative to your body as that of the overhand cast, only you must look at that arc from a different point of view. To be precise, the top of the sidearm arc is perpendicular to the arc of the overhand cast.

Another important similarity shared by the overhand and sidearm casts is that they should be made while you are standing square to your target. Begin with your feet. They should be set facing your target, lined up with your shoulders. This will keep your center of balance in line with your target and will increase the likelihood that your cast will go where you want it to and not into some faraway tree limb instead. You will also want to keep your hands squared with the rest of your body so that you use them to provide power and balance to your cast. If your feet, shoulders, and hands are all in line with each other and you release your cast at the top of its arc, your lure will follow the path you have chosen.

The Backhand Cast

Quite often I find myself fishing up against steep river banks or next to large trees. It becomes nearly impossible to haul back to make either an overhand or sidearm cast, and I must make use of the backhand cast. This is a relatively simple cast which is good for short distances. At first, you may find that you will be sacrificing some accuracy as you get used to the technique. After a little practice, though, the backhand cast should become quite natural to you.

Assume you are on a steep shoreline, looking out at a river or a lake. Stand so that you are directly facing the opposite shore. Turn your head in the direction of your casting hand. This will be the path that you will be attempting to make your cast follow. Next, cock your casting arm by bringing it across your body to your opposite shoulder. Almost all of the backhand cast is delivered by your elbow and wrist. With a quick but smooth motion, you will swing your casting arm away from the shoulder where you cocked it. When you reach the top of the arc, or when your rod tip has appeared directly in front of your face, release the line and continue to follow through until your casting arm is fully extended.

There is a slight variation to this cast which is useful for getting under low-hanging tree limbs. Begin your cast at knee level on the side opposite your casting arm and swing your arm around as before. The one big change in this style of backhand cast is that you allow your casting hand to rise upward a little bit so that when you complete your follow-through, your arm is extended at about waist height. This slight, upward movement will allow your lure to fly in an arc and will prevent your cast from hitting the water too early, causing your cast to land short of its target.

The Flip

The flip is a very simple casting technique which you should be able to master after only a little practice. It is an excellent alternative to the backhand cast, as it requires no backcasting room. It is ideal for delicate presentations at distances of less than 15 feet. The flip is also a perfect way to slip your lure into tight spots like the edges of weed beds, sunken logs, boulder outcroppings, and dense vegetation.

The Flip Cast

Hold your rod tip directly overhead and strip off between 7 and 9 feet of line so that your lure hangs waist high. Then strip off an additional arm's length of line and hold it in your free hand. By dipping the wrist of the hand holding the rod, start to swing the lure like a pendulum back and forth, using your target area as the far end of your swing.

You should not let the lure swing back behind you. Instead, as you begin to create a larger arc with the pendulum motion, tilt your rod tip toward your target to allow for a wider arc. When the lure is at the back part of its arc, closest to you, flip your wrist and allow the line to slip through both your casting hand and the hand holding the extra arm's length of line. Do not let go of the line, though. You need to maintain hand control right up until the lure actually enters the water to prevent it from making a loud splash. Remember, you will be using this cast at extremely close range, and you should therefore endeavor to keep things as quiet as possible.

TWO

The Fish and How to Catch Them on Ultralight

9
Trout

O f all the freshwater species to be discussed in this book, the trout must be considered royalty. These cold-water fish are found in much of the United States and Canada. They are prized for their delicate flavor on the plate and their superb fighting abilities in the water. While there are many kinds of trout, from the Dolly Varden of the Rocky Mountains to the Arctic char of Canada and Northern Europe as well as the lake trout and steelhead, this chapter will focus on the three most sought-after species.

The Species

The first is the rainbow trout (*Oncorhynchus mykiss*)*. This beautiful fish originated in the western United States and Canada and

---

* Many recall when the rainbow trout was classified as *Salmo gairdneri*. Things have gotten a bit more complicated in the species versus subspecies classification debate in recent years. *Trout* magazine reported in their Summer 1990 issue that the rainbow trout and the brown could no longer be deemed part of the same genus. In fact, this remarkable article by Robert J. Behnke asserts that the brown trout and the Atlantic salmon are more closely related than previously thought. Fortunately, Mr. Behnke still maintains that the brook trout is a char. I would point out that the science is continuing to evolve, and it is possible the new names for our old friends in the trout world may be changed again before long.

is well known among freshwater anglers for its spectacular leaping abilities. The rainbow has been successfully stocked all over the world. It survives well in temperatures between 45 and 65 degrees Fahrenheit. It can live in water temperatures of up to 75 degrees, but not for long periods of time. Ideally, the rainbow seeks out water that falls between 50 and 60 degrees.

Brown trout (*Salmo trutta*) were first found in Europe. In the mid-nineteenth century, they were imported to the United States and have adapted very well to life in the New World.

Ultralight gear allows far greater sensitivity as you cast to, hook, and fight trout, while also making a real challenge of your fight with a truly big fish. (Photo by Deane Wheeler.)

Brown are not known for their leaping abilities, but on occasion you will find them taking to the air once they are hooked. Normally, though, brown will lie low in the deeper pools of a river, hunting insects and minnows. These fish can grow large, often exceeding 18 inches in length. They are very territorial, even when they are not spawning.

Brown trout are also extremely cautious fish. Because all trout have extraordinary peripheral vision (they can see 300 degrees around themselves), all the species of this fish are easily spooked by unnatural movement or the presence of moving shadows above them. The brown trout will lie in the slow-moving current, able to detect the slightest movement of an intruder or of a meal. Often a brown will follow an aquatic insect or minnow for 20 or 30 yards before deciding whether or not to attack. They will eat almost anything and have been known to feed on other trout. Brown trout seem to really love a good rainstorm and the silty runoff that results from it. When the river is running high after rain, while the other trout seek out the clearer-running streams of small brooks and upstream tributaries, brown trout will come out of their hiding places and feed with what approaches wild abandon.

The third species we are going to discuss in this chapter is the brook trout (*Salvelinus fontinalis*). The brookie is native to the eastern United States and Canada. It requires extremely cold, pure water for its survival and is by far the most fragile of the three species under discussion. It is not in fact closely related to the other two, being a member of the char family. Other fish in this group include the Dolly Varden (*Salvelinus malma*) of the Rocky Mountains and the Arctic char (*Salvelinus alpinus*), which is native to Alaska, Canada, and northern Europe.

Normally, the brook trout is found in the upper reaches of major rivers, river tributaries, and in remote beaver ponds. The first two of these three locations have cool water, often a good 10 degrees colder than the same rivers farther downstream. Also, since the smaller, upstream sections of rivers tend to be less of a target for land development and construction, the water there runs free of environmental pollutants and silt. These pristine conditions are ideal for the brookie, and it is in areas like these headwaters that it thrives.

Beaver ponds are always likely places to find brook trout. These ponds are built by beavers to dam up a small stream like the tiny tributaries I have just described. The brook trout that inhabit one of these streams become trapped by the dam, and as the flat land around the dam begins to flood, the brookies spread out in the pond that is formed. While they may continue to venture upstream from the pond at the inlet, they rarely pass downstream below the dam again.

Equipment and Lures

When fishing for trout, I like to use the very lightest lines. The Fenwick Liteline is a good one, although you might also want to try Berkley Trilene or Stren® Magnathin. All three of these are small-diameter lines which give you a good chance of working your lure through the water without the fish's detecting the unnatural presence of yards of monofilament leading the lure along. Four-pound test will do you well in almost all circumstances, giving you the extra strength to battle a large fish in a strong current without being so heavy that you won't feel smaller fish strike as well.

The precision of casting that small-diameter line makes possible is also a tremendous aid when you fish for trout during the heat of summer. Normally, the first week of August brings us low water levels and high water temperatures. Both of these conditions bring a great deal of suffering to the trout living in our rivers and streams, and they tend to huddle below submerged boulders. I hit the water in the middle of one August day while the sun was at its absolute highest and found the fish incredibly active. I was using a brand-new ultralight rod that my wife and daughter had given me for my birthday, fixed up with a Number 1 gold Mepps lure. The water was running at just about 69 degrees, warm but not horribly so, and before I knew it, I was into a beautiful foot-long rainbow trout.

My fish did not take to the air as I expected it to, but rather, ran straight upstream and tried to lose itself in the pocket water which ran to my right. I had to be very careful in turning it, as I was using 4-pound-test Magnathin and the rainbow's body was turned against me and the current. By pumping the rod before bringing in line, I was able to tire it out and bring it in.

"Pumping" is a term most closely associated with deep-sea fishing. When working in a large fish like a marlin or a sailfish, an angler will wrestle line away from his quarry by pulling upward on the rod until it stands close to a 90-degree angle from the water's surface. The angler will then quickly begin to reel in line, while at the same time dropping his rod tip, so as not to increase the strain on the line. This pumping action is repeated during any time that the fish has stalled in the water and is unable to run.

I caught and released three more rainbows and a small-mouth bass, all in just about an hour and a half. I also lost three other fish, one of which broke off while it was still a good 30 yards away from me. All in all, a good afternoon of fishing.

In selecting a rod for trout, I go with the smallest one I can get. Generally, I like to keep the length under 5 feet with a slow action. Daiwa, Eagle Claw, and Shimano make good rods in this size, as does Fenwick. I have a preference for a "soft" or flexible tip, as it allows me a little bit slower action when casting my lure into tight places, but as you remember from chapter 4, you should use rods that fit your own style.

Rainbows and browns characteristically make long runs once hooked. During this time, they can take out a considerable amount of line, especially if they weigh much over 1½ pounds. While a true trophy trout may weigh over 4 pounds, do not take the somewhat smaller ones lightly. A 2-pound rainbow can put on an aerial show to rival any tarpon or billfish and can place an enormous strain on your reel. Therefore, I suggest you use great care in selecting the right reel for this species.

One of the things to look for is a well-designed drag system. Many reels today are built with rear drag adjusters as well as the more traditional front adjuster found on top of the spool. This little dial, mounted just behind the handle on the rear-adjusting models, allows the angler to change the tension that holds the line on the reel. Whatever the type of drag adjuster, an angler who has set up the drag incorrectly in the first place is in a lot of trouble before he or she even gets into the water to fish. You should always check the drag on your reel before you start fishing (see chapter 5 on reels).

As you will probably be fishing in moving water for trout, it makes sense to use a reel with as high a gear ratio as possible. Many ultralight reels now feature ratios of better than 5:1, which allows you to bring your lure back through even the fastest of currents without too much trouble. Remember, trout position themselves to face the current, and so cannot see you if you are directly downstream from them. That means your retrieve will be with, rather than against, the current.

To help you in spotting the fish and seeing how it reacts to your lure, I suggest that you wear a pair of polarized sunglasses (see chapter 7). Polarized lenses greatly cut down on glare and will aid you in spotting and following your prey. You will want to keep your eyes on the fish to make sure it sees your lure. If it does not react, try altering the speed of your retrieve or the depth at which you are working.

Trout are naturally selective feeders and as such they will rarely fall for the same trick twice. If the trout does turn to follow your lure but soon afterward pulls away and returns to its original holding position, bring in your lure and change it. I like to start out by using a spoon lure like the Phoebe either in the $\frac{1}{12}$- or $\frac{1}{8}$-ounce size. This small, fish-shaped spoon is bent so that it makes an erratic, wobbling motion as it swims through the water. The flash of the metal can attract trout as well, but the strange movement it makes seems to be the most effective feature of this lure. If I find that fish are following the Phoebe but not striking at it, I will change to a spinning lure like a $\frac{1}{12}$-ounce Rooster Tail, Number 1 Mepps, or a Number 4 Panther Martin. These lures feature a spinning blade at the top which rotates as it moves in the water. The flashing of the blade and the low buzzing noise it creates are key to the success of these lures in catching fish.

I was guiding on the Winooski River in Bolton, Vermont, one cold, rainy day in May and saw a good-sized mayfly hatch occurring. Swallows were swooping all over the river's surface feeding on these emerging insects, as was a healthy population of rainbow trout. The fish were lying in the calm backwater behind large boulders and in protected inlets, waiting for food to drift past them. In spite of the extreme cold of the water (my own readings found it to be 48 degrees, unseasonably cool), these trout were very active.

I was fly-fishing that day, and by using an attractor pattern like a Royal Wulff, I successfully caught several of these rainbows, while the three anglers I was guiding did quite well with brown trout using ⅛-ounce Phoebe lures on their ultralight rigs, fished at a depth of about 2 feet and cranked in at a slow speed. The browns tended to follow the lure for several yards before striking, as is their custom. Brown trout are very wary creatures and are slow to initiate an attack. The rainbows, however, were less careful and often took the small spoon within seconds of its landing in the water.

I also guide a lot of fishing trips on the Dog River in Northfield, Vermont. It is a small river, but it holds some of the biggest brown trout I know of. When the river turns muddy, these huge fish—some of them in the 5- and 6-pound range—will zip around the larger pools and feed on the surface for terrestrial insects that have been swept off the shoreline by the runoff. I do best under these circumstances by fishing a small streamer with a vibrating blade right under the surface. Worden's Spinning Fly is a good bet for this type of strategy. Another alternative is the Kastmaster lure, an irregularly shaped spoon made by Acme, the same company that makes the Phoebe.

Top water lures can also be an option for you, especially at dusk when the really big trout start to feed after sleeping away the heat of the day. Sinking and deep-diving crankbaits can be very effective, too, particularly on large brown trout. Rapala makes a whole range of floating lures and crankbaits, as does Bagley. Rapala's Mini Fat Trap and Countdown are very good, as are Bagley's Bang-O lure and the Bitty B. Most folks associate these kinds of lures with bass, but trout anglers can do equally well with them, provided they recognize the different ways that each of the three kinds of trout hunt and defend their territories. The key is to keep loose, maintain an open mind regarding lure selection, and be ready to try just about anything when it comes to varying your retrieve.

Stalking Trout

There are a few general rules for you to remember, regardless of where you plan to stalk these fish and what lures you have packed along. The first is that trout have exceedingly good eyesight. As I have already mentioned, their peripheral vision is remarkable. The only things they cannot see are objects directly in back of them. This is one of two reasons why it is important to approach any new pool on a river from downstream. As trout rest in the river flow facing upstream, they have a perfect view of any food which the current might sweep past them. Upon spotting a fish in the river, you should aim to cast over its head, landing your lure 15 to 20 feet upstream from where it is lying. Then let it ride back down to the fish on the current.

Heat and glare are important factors to take into consideration in pursuing trout. One very hot day in August, I had a great afternoon of rainbow fishing by working the riffle water at the tops of large rapids. In spite of the high temperatures and glaring sunlight, these fish were hitting because they had a good oxygen supply, and I was working my lure right through it, using the small-diameter line which effectively hid itself from the trout. When water temperatures start to rise, stream fish will seek out places where the water runs a little faster over submerged rocks and boulders. This riffling action causes oxygen to be absorbed by the water, and this manifests itself as bubbles frothing up on the surface. Fish will naturally congregate at these parts of the river during the summer in an effort to eke out some relief from the suffocating effects of the tepid water. Another plus for the fish is that the turbulence caused by the water washing over the larger rock formations serves up a bounty of food in the form of insect nymphs being swept off their safe havens on the rock faces.

By casting into the wakes of rocks and the small riffles, an angler can position his lure in the most probable spot for it to encounter a fish. This type of precision casting is made far easier by using the small-diameter lines because they unspool off your reel with little friction, thereby making your cast more accurate.

Sometimes fish will strike at your lure not as food but

because they feel it has come to invade their territory. Given the heat I experienced that day in August, I think this is most likely what was happening. These trout were not feeding at all. Rather, they were defending the protected areas they had staked out for themselves from a perceived interloper. I found my best strikes came when I cast directly across the moving water and retrieved as my lure swung around downstream from me.

Trout have good hearing. When fishing for them, use great care in how you move through the water. Water, being denser than air, conducts sound for long distances very well. This is

Because trout can run, dive, and jump, thereby twisting and damaging your line, you really need to be on top of every change in tactics the fish throws at you.

another reason for approaching your fish from downstream, as the river current will tend to push the sound of your movement back past you before it has the chance to travel upstream to the fish. But even all this stealth is wasted if you blunder in your cast, retrieve, or setting of the hook.

There are a number of effective ways of correctly positioning yourself in a trout stream. One method is to wade in and plant yourself directly downstream from the pool you aim to fish. Make a simple overhand cast by bringing your rod tip back to the two o'clock position behind you and casting forward, releasing at approximately ten o'clock. This is a fairly standard way to fish for rainbow trout, as rainbows prefer to feed in the middle of the faster-moving riffles and at the tops of runs where there is a bit more current moving past them. If there are obstructions in your way—say a stray tree limb or low-lying shrub—you may be forced to make a sidearm cast. In this case, tilt your rod perpendicular to your body and use the same two o'clock/ten o'clock position to effect your cast.

Sometimes an overhang or a fallen tree that has nestled itself in the middle of a run can make casting from directly downstream impossible. In these cases, a quick review of your high school geometry can be most helpful. After all, the antique name for fishing is "angling," and so it makes sense to look at unusual casting situations as geometric problems. Try to look at the top of the run as the top point of a triangle with the position immediately downstream as the bottom point. By moving up onto the shore and cautiously walking upstream, you can often cut down on the angle preventing you from casting into the upstream side of the obstruction.

When the water runs under an embankment, brook trout do an interesting thing that requires careful positioning and casting on your part. They like to hide up against the banks of small streams, in the cuttings made by the current. When a stream erodes the bank near heavy shrub or tree root growth, it creates a small indentation that the brook trout will swim into and use as a vantage point. They can keep out of the way of larger predators while staying well within range of food swept past them by the current. Trout like to at least try to stay near the main current, which acts as a feeding lane through which all manner of insects are swept.

To get to a brook trout when it is hiding under a cut bank, you should try to stand perpendicular to the bank. Flip over the bail to your ultralight reel, lightly grasp the line in your free hand, bring the rod tip straight up, and gently let the lure swing like a pendulum in front of you. When the lure begins to swing toward your target, lightly snap your wrist with the momentum you have created with the lure and release the line you hold in your free hand. If you practice this a while before taking to the stream, the lure will arc in the direction of your target—namely, the cut bank—and will land within reach of the fish. This flipping technique does take some time to get used to, but it is very effective for short casts. (See chapter 8 for a more detailed description and illustration of the flip.)

Reacting to Strikes

Another important part of successful trout fishing is reacting to the fish's attack, setting the hook once the trout strikes your lure. More often than not, the trout will spot your lure upstream from where it is lying, follow it for a short distance, and then, if it chooses to, attack the lure from the rear. Trout do not actually taste the metal of your hook at first. Instead, they taste the water surrounding it. If they do not recognize the taste, if it has more of a metallic flavor than a small minnow, say, they will spit it out. The fish will breathe in your lure, taste it, and exhale it in less than one second. Because trout are selective feeders, they will often refuse to feed again for a period of time should you miss their strike.

Setting the hook on a trout is done delicately. When you feel the fish pull on your line, pull upward on the line with your arm as though you were picking up a glass of water, but add a small snap at the elbow just as your arm reaches a 30-degree angle with the water's surface. The rising movement of your arm is not what sets the hook; this only brings in the minute amount of slack that naturally occurs while you retrieve. The quick snap of your elbow, acting as the fulcrum to this geometric pattern, is what actually drives the hook home into the fish's jaw.

Brook trout, while somewhat selective, are normally the least so of the three trout under discussion. Many times I have missed a striking brookie with a small lure only to have it hit again on a different lure on the very next cast. This tells me that brook trout are not all that wary. A rainbow trout, however, may not feed on anything for up to a couple of hours if it feels the nick of a hook, and a brown will often abandon hunting altogether if it becomes spooked or suspicious.

Brookies also strike somewhat differently from other trout when they feed. The brown and the rainbow will attack their prey either head-on or from the rear. They specialize in running down smaller fish and aquatic insects, and so they will almost always attempt to intercept their prey from their downstream position. When they are in a feeding frenzy, rainbows and browns will attack your lure from the front and the rear, with their bodies running perpendicular to the river bottom.

Brook trout, on the other hand, attack by turning sideways to the lure just as they open their jaws to strike. This will actually flip them downward, toward the river bottom, as they strike, causing them to miss their prey on occasion. I have fished for brookies on beaver ponds and in small streams and watched as they bumped against my lure unsuccessfully several times before actually taking it into their mouths. It is a comical sight to watch these very determined little fish fiercely bat themselves against my "escaping" lure.

Playing the Fish

Fighting trout is different from doing battle with almost any other type of fish. Trout have very soft mouths, containing little bone to hold your hook. This means that you must not horse a trout in, as it is likely that you will tear the hook right out of its mouth by doing so. One of the reasons why ultralight gear is so beautifully suited to trout fishing is its sensitive touch. You will feel the hit, the hook-set, and the direction in which your fish has decided to run far better using ultralight than with heavier rigs. Use this to your advantage while recognizing the constraints of the equipment. Ultralight equipment is perfect for taking big trout because it offers the angler a unique ability to feel all the delicate subtleties of a fight and use them to his advantage. Because trout can run, dive, and jump, thereby twisting and damaging your line, you really need to be on top of every change the fish throws at you.

For example, brown trout employ a funny trick once hooked, one which the largemouth bass also like to play on anglers. They will stick to the bottom of the river and seek out a ledge or a boulder to line up against. Then, while they put pressure on your line, they will work their mouths against the rock, rubbing the line on the rough surface in an attempt to weaken it. If you doubt that so low a life form as a fish would be sophisticated enough to use its surroundings as a tool, let me tell you a story.

While I was guiding a client of mine on a river that was known for its big brown trout, he hooked into a real beauty at the base of a large waterfall. The client was using a 4½-foot ultralight rod with 4-pound-test line and a ⅛-ounce silver Kastmaster lure. The brown took the lure and immediately shot off toward the open water in the middle of the big pool below the falls. After several wide sweeps around the pool, it pulled up alongside a submerged rock ledge and refused to move. I instructed the client to apply a little extra pressure on the fish and to try to steer it back out into open water. The fish complied but returned to the ledge within a few seconds.

From my vantage point on a rock overlooking the whole scene, I could see that the fish was rubbing the left side of its jaw, the side where the hook was buried, against the ledge. I cautioned my client on this development, and he again put pressure on the fish. The trout took another wide sweep of the pool but came back to the ledge once more and continued rubbing against the rock.

The client worked the fish out into the open again and then began to work it back toward us. This was a risky thing to do because it required him to strain his already weakened line. However, he had been able to feel the fish tire through the light line, and we soon had it at our feet. As I reached down and pulled the fish out of the water by its tail, the line gave out and snapped. I held an exhausted 4-pound brown trout as my client looked at the broken line in astonishment.

In summary, ultralight gear allows far greater sensitivity as you cast to, hook, and fight trout while also making a real challenge of your fight with a truly big fish. While this runs true for all of the species discussed in this book, it is perhaps most true for trout. Ultralight equipment allows you the versatility you will need when dealing with three types of trout that exhibit quite different behavior. This is important, as you are apt to run across rainbows, browns, and brookies all in the same piece of water.

10
Bass

I have guided a lot of bass fishing trips over the years. One July morning, a client of mine and I headed out to a small lake where I had been having some exceptional luck during the spring and early summer. The water was calm, and we had a nice overcast sky to keep things cool. The water temperature was about 68, and everything looked perfect for a good day on the water.

We began by fishing along the brushy shoreline, tossing our surface plugs among the weeds and lily pads. We got some decent-sized fish right off, mostly by twitching small Number 7 Rapalas and Bagley's Bang-O crankbaits along the top of the water with a slow, erratic motion. As we headed into the deeper water toward the middle, though, we noticed a good deal of surface action in the heavier weed beds. We switched to weedless hooks with small strips of pork rind attached to them and got several good fish by dragging them over the top of the beds before we made the most startling discovery of the day.

As we reached the outer edge of one large weed bed, I noticed some small baitfish jumping about 100 yards ahead of our position. While we kept working the weeds for fish, I kept looking over at the smaller baitfish to monitor their progress.

Then it happened. There was a sudden explosion of water and the baitfish scattered in a thousand directions at once.

I paddled us out of the weeds, and we chased the rapidly moving school of baitfish until we were within casting range. Jack, my client that day, landed a good cast just over them and began to retrieve his lure. Almost the instant it passed through the school, he got a strike, and about two minutes later he was into a healthy, 2-pound largemouth bass. I had had a great deal of trouble handling these fish, since I had spooled my reel with ultrathin line hoping to compensate for the flood of sunshine that had come once the cloud cover above us broke in the middle of the morning. I had been able to hook into fish readily, but then had had a tough time holding the larger bass as they easily broke my line off by fouling it on submerged roots and dead trees.

After losing several good fish, I solved the problem by switching to a larger-diameter, more elastic line. I still got plenty of strikes, too, once we located the bass feeding on that school of baitfish. The subtleties of light line were completely lost on these greedy fish as they slashed away at almost everything that moved through their path, including our lures. It simply had not been necessary for me to use light line to fool these bass into striking. Indeed, given their size and the subsurface obstructions available to them to aid their escape, it had been a mistake to select a light line.

The bass had been corralling the baitfish in a circular movement that kept the smaller fish from escaping. Every once in a while, the bass would surge into the center of the school and attack, causing the bait to scatter in a desperate attempt to avoid being eaten. Jack's small Kastmaster lure had excited the bass, as it had appeared to be an escaping baitfish, prompting an immediate strike.

But the baitfish and the bass kept moving, and in order to keep up with them, Jack and I had to paddle madly. From time to time, the fish would simply disappear, only to reemerge a short distance away from us. Every time we cast into their midst, we got a strike, and so the chase proved to be both exciting and rewarding. After over an hour, the big school submerged one last time and never resurfaced. A good thing, too, as we were both exhausted.

This story illustrates perhaps the most important single piece of advice I can offer concerning bass fishing. No matter how well proven a specific angling method is, be willing to abandon it immediately should the fishing slow down or conditions change. Bass react to a variety of stimuli in varied ways, so it pays to keep your mind open to new ideas when you are out on the water.

Bass may be the most popular freshwater game fish in North America. In fact, with the increasing attention given to the peacock bass of South and Central America, it is possible that bass will soon become the most pursued freshwater species in the western hemisphere, if not the world. I remember once reading that if the trout and salmon are the elite of fish, then the bass must be the blue-collar equivalent. This is in no way meant as a

Since bass react to a variety of stimuli in varied ways, it pays to keep your mind open to new ideas when you are on the water.

slight to these proud fighting fish or to the anglers who love them. It is simply an acknowledgment that bass are everywhere and available to everyone.

In the continental United States, there is usually a place where an angler can cast into bass-inhabited water within a 20-minute drive from his or her home. They are warm-water dwellers and can tolerate a wide range of temperatures.

The largemouth bass (*Micropterus salmoides*) is an extremely aggressive fish and like its close relative the smallmouth bass (*Micropterus dolomieui*) is spring spawning. During the months of April, May, and June, bass will move out of the shallow water they normally inhabit and pair off for mating.

Ask ten bass anglers what works best at a given time of year, and I promise you at least twelve different answers. With this rather artful disclaimer, I am ready to make a few suggestions based on my own experiences.

Tackle for Bass

If you like using light line, especially 4-pound test, when you work for smallmouth bass, I suggest you lay off the ultrathin types and respool your reel with something that has a bit of stretch like Stren®. Smallmouth can pull awfully hard on line, and the extra give this particular line has can really work to your advantage. Line gets twisted easily just from bringing your lure through the water—not to mention what a good fish can do to it. You should consider changing that line after every 24 hours of actual use, if not more often, just to be on the safe side.

I usually set up two rods when I go lake fishing in my canoe. I will string up a short, 4½-foot rod with 4-pound-test light line for jigging and a 5½- to 6½-foot rod with 6-pound test for crankbaits and spinnerbaits. While I do take a lot of bass on spoons worked along the grassy shorelines and shallows during spawning season, the vast majority of my success with these fish has been either down deep with jigs, at middle depths with diving crankbaits, or right on the surface with top water crankbaits.

Jigging

Of the three methods, jigging seems to be the best all-around way of taking bass. It requires a deft touch, however, and is not as easy as it might appear. The secret is to bounce your ⅛- or ¼-ounce jig off the bottom and to feel the light *tick* of the fish's take. The use of a small-diameter line is crucial to your success, as you do your fishing entirely by feel. As I have already mentioned, I rig up my smallest ultralight rod with light line for jigging. This allows me to feel the hit with far greater sensitivity than I would have were I to use a heavier line on a larger rod.

Jigs come in several varieties, but they are always lead-headed hooks that are dressed either with feathers, plastic, or a combination of the two. The Marabou jig is a very popular choice for bass. This feather-dressed jig undulates as it bounces through the water, appearing to be either a leech or an injured baitfish. Another good choice is the jig and plastic grub. The grub is placed on the jig by piercing its thick head with the tip of the jig's hook and then running the hook inside the grub until the shank of the hook is completely hidden. You then turn the tip of the hook downward so that it protrudes from the bottom of the grub. There are varying lengths of grubs. Some are barely longer than the shank of the jig hook, while others will run to 4 or even 6 inches long. The longer ones often feature flattened tails that move provocatively as the jig is pulled through the water.

Regardless of what design of jig you use, the basic strategy for fishing it is the same. Cast your jig out toward a point, a rock outcropping, or some other structure and allow it to completely sink to the bottom. Once it has stopped moving, give your rod tip a sharp twitch and reel in the slack. Allow your jig to rest on the bottom again and continue to repeat this action until you can no longer reach the bottom with the line you have left. Your jig will appear to hop along the bottom of the lake, and that action is what will attract the bass.

You may not feel a great pull on the end of your line when a bass strikes your jig or grub. Instead, you will feel only a light tug—a *tick*, as I have previously described it. Do not be deceived by the lightness of the strike. I have caught plenty of 3- and 4-pound bass that felt more like a 6-inch perch tapping on my line than a healthy, mature bass. The bass will open its mouth and inhale your jig, quickly tasting the water surrounding it to make sure it is good to eat. If it feels something is not right, the bass will exhale your jig as quickly as it took it. This means you must react quickly to any kind of tap you feel through the line, no matter how slight.

The downside to jigging is that you are very apt to get snagged on the bottom. There is not too much you can do about this. Jigs are supposed to be worked on the bottom, and getting snagged is just one of the prices of going fishing with them. I really cannot offer you very much in the way of advice here. You could try using jigs fitted with a weed guard, a small piece of wire that runs from the hook eyelet down to the tip of the point. While not a foolproof gimmick, the weed guard will help to prevent you from hanging up on weed growth, logs, and rocks.

Fishing for bass from a canoe is incomparable sport. The canoe allows you to cover long stretches of shoreline almost noiselessly, providing you with plenty of opportunities to hook into a big one.

(Fortunately, jigs are not very expensive and are extremely easy to make. See the section on jigs in chapter 6 for more information.)

Top Water Lures

For more bone-thumping strikes, nothing in the world beats a top water lure. Jitterbugs, Rapalas, Bagley Bang-Os, and Rebels are all fine examples of this kind of crankbait used for bass. You must be sure of two things when you select your crankbait, though, so as to insure you will get the action you want.

First, make sure your crankbait is a floating lure and not one designed to sink. This may seem obvious, but it really is not as simple as it sounds. Floating and sinking crankbaits look almost exactly alike and can be differentiated best by checking the packaging as you browse your favorite tackle shop. Floaters and sinkers are clearly labeled, and you should keep your eyes open for these designations.

Second, try to buy floating crankbaits with very short bills. The bill is the forward portion of the lure that extends downward, just under the painted eyes. Most crankbaits are painted up to look like minnows, and the size of the eyes is usually just a little larger than life to attract fish from a distance. The bill is the portion of the crankbait that regulates how deep it will dive when retrieved at a moderate pace. A short bill will make a very shallow dive, and these baits are the ones you will want to concentrate on using when fishing on the water's surface.

Crankbaits fished on the surface for bass are usually retrieved fairly slowly, so as to prevent the bill from dragging the lure underwater. Twitch the rod so as to make your bait duck briefly underwater an inch or so and then bob back up to the top. Let the lure rest for a second and repeat, always bringing in your slack as you go. The bass will erupt from underneath the crankbait, making the strike extremely obvious.

Diving and Underwater Lures

If you use a longer-billed or diving crankbait for bass, your strategy changes somewhat. The faster you bring in your line, the quicker the bait will dive before finally reaching its cruising depth. I usually experiment with different lengths of bills and different speeds until I can figure out what the bass are hitting. Then I settle into that one depth and speed. Diving crankbaits are extremely useful for working long drop-offs, dams, gradually sloping shorelines, and points. As your lure will be several feet below the surface, strikes are indicated entirely by feel. However, unlike the subtle *tick* you experience when fishing a jig or even a plastic worm, there will be an obvious strike if your lure is taken. Bass wallop a crankbait with great zeal.

Another worthwhile method of fishing for bass is with a spinnerbait. Spinnerbaits feature a whirling blade on the tip of a piece of wire that has been twisted at a right angle. At the end of the opposite tip is the hook, to which bass fishermen may fasten a grub, pork rind, plastic skirt, or even a plastic worm. Spinnerbaits are fished in two distinct ways, one resembling jigging, the other more like handling a conventional spinning lure.

Jigging a spinnerbait off the bottom requires the same skills as using a regular jig. The one big difference is that spinnerbaits are usually retrieved extremely slowly. You allow the spinnerbait to sink completely to the bottom and then slowly raise your rod tip from a nine o'clock to a twelve o'clock position, causing the bait to rise erratically off the bottom. Once you have reached the twelve o'clock position, drop your rod tip and allow the lure to settle back to the bottom, bringing in your slack to keep the line taut. If you find yourself fishing for prespawning bass in the spring, a very effective way to work a spinnerbait can be to cast it into the shallows and retrieve it quickly along the water's surface. The blade will rotate at a very high speed, emitting a buzzing noise that will arouse the curiosity of any bass in the area.

In all cases, try to use lures that are no more than ¼ ounce in weight. In fact, when dealing with any lure other than a spinnerbait or a crankbait, it is advisable to stick to a weight of ⅛ ounce or less. Remember, your ultralight rod was built to cast very small objects. With some of the floating crankbaits, you can bump up to ⅜ ounce, but endeavor to keep heavier lures to a minimum. You can put excess stress on your rod tip and cause it to snap if you are not careful.

Color Selection

Color selection of my bass lures is made pretty easy for me on most trips. On days when there is even the hint of sunlight, I stick to colors like green and black. However, on wet, rainy days, I get to go a little wild and use bright oranges, reds, and yellows. The flash of color when the weather goes bleak seems to entice fish. Low atmospheric pressure does affect bass; they can become quite sulky when the barometer bottoms out as a front passes through.

Favorite Bass Habitat

A favorite haunt of bass are the many reservoirs in this country that provide electrical power through hydroelectric dams. The dams themselves often make extremely good bass habitat, as they form an even and gradual slope where bass will congregate. Smallmouth bass like to hang suspended right at the edge of drop-offs, and the contour of the power dam's slope is just one huge drop-off in their eyes. Furthermore, many of the power dams constructed during the 1930s by the Civilian Conservation Corps were hand-built from stones that could be easily handled by light trucks and laborers. Smallmouth bass absolutely love these rocky formations. There is an abundance of food there in the way of crayfish, schools of minnows, and insect nymphs. The crevices between the rocks also make for ideal hiding places. For the smallmouth, then, a good-sized power dam is a condo development with a built-in supermarket.

About the only downside to power dams is that the fish that live in their reservoirs can become injured when water is let through the turbines. A reservoir of, say, 800 square acres with an 80- to 100-foot-high dam can fluctuate by 2 feet or more based on just a few hours of prolonged water withdrawal. The dropping of the water level will usually drive bass living in the shallows a good 10 to 15 feet deeper than normal and can scatter densely packed groups of fish as well. This means that you may have trouble locating large groups of bass that were at a depth of 10 feet along a drop-off on one day when the water starts to go down the day after. It is a good idea to call the dam operator and ask what the withdrawal schedule is for the days around your planned fishing trip.

Riprap formations also make for excellent smallmouth habitat. Here, large rocks are dumped down an embankment to reinforce the shoreline and to help resist erosion. The submerged rocks often form large crevices which can house equally large bass. Some of your best fishing opportunities will be found when you come upon these artificial formations or natural rock outcroppings.

Another good bet for both large- and smallmouth bass are submerged structures like trees, points, or even manmade objects like houses. When large dams are constructed, the government often takes land by eminent domain and then floods it to create the reservoir. If you can find them, old maps showing the position of houses, barns, towers, or roads, now submerged, can prove to be extremely valuable. Bass often congregate around these structures and will use them as homes and hunting grounds.

Largemouths have a great affection for the tangles of submerged brush, brushy shorelines, lily pad beds, and heavily weed-infested waters. One of the obvious reasons for this preference is the hiding places these locations offer. But not so obvious is the shelter these kinds of spots can provide against climbing temperatures in the summertime. Water under a weed bed or any other vegetation can be 10 degrees cooler than the water just 10 yards out in the open. This can make an enormous difference to your fishing on hot days. The trick to fishing for bass under these circumstances is to watch the surface for any telltale movement. Weeds are far denser than water, and when they move, you can be sure a good-sized fish caused it. Be careful, though, when fishing in weed beds. Avoid brown-colored weeds, as they will not be emitting the oxygen that healthy greens will. Fish cannot live in low-oxygenated water and will stay away from places where breathing is tough.

Steep cliffs are also very good places to seek out bass. During warm weather, bass will slip from depths of between 10 and 25 feet to levels nearer 40 or 50 feet. They do this to seek out the shade these large rock formations offer, and will hold at varying depths.

In the fall, bass will also move into the deeper water to wait out the winter in a state similar to hibernation as the cold water slows down their metabolic rate. While bass still move about and feed during the chill of winter, they prefer to stay down deep, as the water there can actually be a bit warmer. Once the surface temperature of a lake hits 39 degrees in the late fall, this top layer of water will sink to the lake bottom, forming a thermal layer of warmer water that will remain there until the spring thaw. This water is somewhat denser than the rest of the lake, and fish will move in and out of it throughout the winter months. Once the ice on the surface melts off in the spring, the thermal layer at the bottom will rise to the surface, as will many of the fish that have wintered there.

For the purposes of the ultralight angler seeking fish in the warmer months of the year, it is best to remember that both

Any type of vegetation makes ideal cover for bass escaping from the heat during midsummer.

small- and largemouth bass seek shelter in similar ways, although smallmouth have a preference for rocks and largemouth are happiest near dense vegetation. Largemouth bass are plentiful during the summer, and the heat seems to make them especially aggressive. Most anglers do well by using Hula Poppers or Jitterbugs, which are varieties of top water crankbaits. Cast your lure out into the edges of heavy bank growth and let it sit still until you can't see the ripples made from its landing. As soon as the water is completely still, twitch your bait slightly and pull in any slack. Largemouths will often hit on the first or second twitch, right on the surface.

During spawning season, though, bass seem to lose much of their affection for dense cover and will move out of their lairs and up into the shallows of the water they inhabit. Females will dig out nests in the sand and lay their eggs, while the male stands guard to prevent interlopers or any other challenging male bass from getting too near. Once the female has finished, he will fertilize the eggs. Bass will protect their beds for a time after the eggs have been laid, too, ensuring that the young have ample opportunity to hatch and survive. It is during this time that these fish are most vulnerable. I would urge you not to disturb bass sitting on their nests. Many aquatic scavengers may attack an unguarded bed, wiping out the season's spawning efforts.

River Bass

River smallmouth react to cover much the same way their counterparts in lakes do. The stone bridges which span rivers are particularly good spots to hit. Try casting into the shadows under the bridges, as they provide the bass with protection from light and heat and also afford them the hiding places that large structures can offer. Riprap, the outflow of power dams, and submerged boulders are other favorite haunts. I suggest anglers use lures like the Panther Martin or Mepps. Smallmouths can be extremely active during the afternoon once the shadows of the trees begin to fall over the river.

Bass are exciting fish in that they exhibit a wide variety of behavior and will always keep you guessing as to what they might be hitting. Another point is that once you have discovered what they have keyed in on during any particular day, you can stick with that strategy until weather or water conditions change. Bass also like to group together, which means that if you find one, you are apt to be in close proximity to others. If you catch a bass on a flat that is shaded by an overhanging tree on a shallow-diving crankbait, release that bass and get your line back out there as quickly as you can. The odds are you will be into another before too long.

11

Salmon and Lake Trout

Perhaps the most prized of all fish is the salmon. Salmon are a valuable commodity, as evidenced by the enormous demand for their flesh in the American, European, and Asian marketplace. They are also one of the most highly sought-after game fish in the world. Anglers from all over the globe travel to Alaska, the Canadian Maritimes, New Zealand, Ireland, and Norway to cast their lines for these fabled fish.

In North America, there are six major species of salmon. Five of them inhabit the waters of the Pacific Ocean and its river tributaries. They are the chinook or king salmon (*Oncorhynchus tshawytscha*), the sockeye salmon (*Oncorhynchus nerka*), the coho or silver salmon (*Oncorhynchus kisutch*), the chum or dog salmon (*Oncorhynchus keta*), and the pink or humpy salmon (*Oncorhynchus gorbuscha*). In Atlantic waters, the Atlantic salmon (*Salmo salar*) reigns alone. The popular landlocked salmon is identical to the Atlantic except that it inhabits lakes and other inland waters separate from the sea.

For hundreds of years, the only way an angler might acceptably catch salmon was with a fly rod. For many anglers, the same is true today. However, for the truly adventurous piscator, there are few thrills that rival the feeling of a leaping salmon, caught by a tiny ⅛-ounce lure, being warily handled on 4- or 6-

pound-test line. The ancient sport of salmon fishing has finally caught up to the twenty-first-century technology of ultralight angling.

Describing salmon fishing to someone who has never done it is very difficult. Yes, it is a little like trout fishing in that both trout and salmon are members of the salmonid family of fish. In many ways, salmon and trout do resemble one another, and some would even argue that steelhead trout and salmon are virtually the same due to their great size and leaping abilities, and also due to the great difficulty experienced in catching them. But in many ways, this misses the point. Salmon fishing is different from any other type of fishing because the salmon is essentially the most challenging, exciting, and rewarding fish to pursue.

Tackle for Salmon

You will want to use a good strong reel. Shimano's Symetre 1000 and Stradic 1000 are as good choices as any I can think of, although the Daiwa SS700 Tournament and Daiwa Samuri Long Cast 700 and 705 are also well built for the punishment that a fast-running salmon can inflict on your equipment. All these reels fall within the definition of ultralight, but they are somewhat heavier than most, ranging from 7 to almost 9 ounces.

The big difference between the Daiwa and Shimano reels here is the gear ratio. While all three Daiwas boast perfectly serviceable 4.4:1 to 4.9:1 ratios, both Shimano reels offer an astonishing 6:1. Abu Garcia also makes a very fine reel called the Cardinal Pro Max, which features a 5.4:1 gear ratio. Abu Garcia's Cardinal Gold Max also has the same numbers. The Abu Garcia reels are extremely compact, which is desirable, and both weigh about 7½ ounces, making them powerful packages.

Gear ratio is very important in salmon fishing, as these fish will attain speeds of up to 60 miles per hour during their pursuit of your bait and the subsequent fight. When a big fish rushes you, you must be ready to pull in huge amounts of line in an extremely short period of time. On the other hand, it is equally important that your reel be ready to give back that line, either by back-reeling or with a sufficiently strong drag.

A long stiff-action rod is going to be your best ally. There are plenty of good ones to choose from. The St. Croix Legend comes in a 7-foot length, two-piece, which is perfect for salmon fishing. It has a moderate to fast action and will stand up well against the fast-running salmon and the powerful lake trout. Fenwick's HMG rod is quite nice, too. It comes in a 6-foot length and is a one-piece. All Star's 6-footer is also an excellent choice.

In choosing a fishing line for salmon, you will want to power up. Start with 6-pound test unless you plan on trolling, in which case you should choose 8-pound. Stren® is great stuff and will give just a little when the fish jumps or runs. If you are going to be fishing in very clear water, try Berkley Trilene UltraThin. This small-diameter line is surprisingly tough and can take quite a lot of strain. Other good lines for salmon and lakers are Berkley TriMax, Bagley's Silver Thread, and Fenwick River Line.

Lures for Salmon

Salmon will respond best to lures with a lot of flash. This makes spoons a most logical choice. The Mooselook Wobbler is an excellent selection. You will notice that this spoon lure is quite broad and therefore reflects a good deal of light as it works through the water. While I am a big fan of the Phoebe and the Kastmaster, I have to admit that there are other lures that work just a little better for salmon. The classic Dardevle is a good choice. Like the Mooselook Wobbler, it is a broad spoon lure with a lot of flash. Normally, though, the Dardevle is colored red and white. I like to paint over this pattern when I go salmon fishing, usually with a chrome-colored paint.

Another classic salmon selection for ultralight spin-fishing is a streamer fly. "A streamer fly?" I hear you ask with some dismay. Yes, this book is about ultralight spinning gear, but that does not mean we cannot experiment with some unorthodox methods. Streamers work beautifully with ultralight gear and can be especially effective on salmon.

I have a good friend named Deane Wheeler who does some unique things to his lures and flies when he goes out trolling for salmon. On one fishing trip I took with him, Deane had tied up a few Number 2 and Number 4 streamers that he'd learned recently. They were tied to a long-shank hook and featured lots of Mylar as well as plenty of purple hackle which Deane had dyed himself at home. He had also done a little doctoring of some of the silver Mooselook Wobblers we were to use. He had put a thin strip of masking tape down the center of the fronts and backs of a few of them and then spraypainted the whole lure the same shade of purple as his scud variants. Before he removed the tape, revealing a bright silver stripe in the middle of the now purple lures, he rubbed some fine steel wool all over the surface of each Wobbler. When he was finished he had a perfect imitation of his scud, painted onto the Mooselook Wobbler.

Let us assume you are planning on doing some trolling in a large lake just after the time when it has iced out in the spring.

Salmon and lake trout are fall spawners, and it makes good sense to let these fish go about their business once you have successfully boated or landed them during the autumn months.

Salmon can be extremely active right after ice out, as they come up to the surface to get at the fresh supply of oxygen. For a short period of time, these fish become absolutely giddy and will leap all over the surface of the water with the burst of energy they receive from the increased oxygen in their blood. They will also feed during this time and are particularly fond of smelt. Therefore, any smelt-pattern streamer will be deadly on salmon if you can find them while they are in this uninhibited state.

Simply set your boat at a fairly crisp trolling speed, say 5 or 6 miles an hour, tie a Number 2- or 4-sized long-shank smelt streamer directly onto your line, and pay out 100 to 150 feet of line. The fly will sink a bit, say a foot or so below the surface, due mainly to the weight of the line. This is perfect cruising depth for salmon. Do not be afraid of trolling too fast, as these fish can build up terrific speed when they key in on a target. Interestingly enough, this same strategy works well on lake trout during the spring. Lakers will have gone through the same kind of semidormant winter as the salmon and are just as eager to get at the smelt and the fresh air.

Of course, the most dramatic salmon fishing takes place once the salmon move into the river tributaries of their lake or ocean homes. It also can be a little intimidating.

I was working on a magazine story one spring and drove to a river just at the Canadian border where the landlocked salmon seasonally run. I hooked up with the photographer who had been hired to take the pictures for this feature on the banks of the stream, and we took a few minutes to scope the situation out before we began. Salmon were moving into the small stream there, even though the water temperature was only about 42 degrees. While we did not spot any really big fish, we saw plenty in the 18- to 20-inch range. While the photographer set up his camera and tripod at the water's edge, I waded into the river and began to cast.

In spite of the layers of clothing I wore beneath my waders, the water's cold sank into my legs quickly. After about a half-hour, my legs were getting that prickly sensation that warns of numbing. I looked up at the shoreline and—nearly fell flat on my face in the water!

The photographer quickly realized I was in some sort of trouble. He stood up from his crouched position behind the tripod and asked whether I was okay. I allowed as I was and explained that I had just been taken out at the knees by one of the larger salmon. The fish had struck my right knee while heading upstream, panicked, and in its fright had run smack into my left leg as it tried to get away from me. The effect was similar to the successful sack of a quarterback in football. These fish had been feeding on the smelt they had followed into the river, and as far as that one salmon was concerned, I was merely an impediment to the task at hand, not any sort of threat to its life. It was a humbling experience.

Salmon running in rivers will react to very few distractions. It is therefore vital that you make sure your lure gets in the way of the fish's progress as much as possible. No subtle presentation or exact imitations are needed for this kind of fishing, particularly during the fall spawning run. In fact, the more bombastic your approach, the better.

I find that spoon lures work best in these cases, although I have also had some measure of success with jigs. However, many states will not allow you to use weighted hooks while salmon are spawning, and this rule will effectively eliminate the jig from your arsenal. I also have done well with streamer flies. You will have to weight the line with a piece of split shot, though, to make your cast. Again, however, some states will not even let you use a weight on a line during the spawning run, and you should double-check the regulations in your area before you try this. If you are not permitted to use any kind of weight on your line or the hook, an unweighted fly can be used on an ultralight rig if you use a little imagination.

The simplest way to cast an unweighted fly with a spinning rod is to let the river do the work for you. Flick the fly into the current below you and allow the line to unspool itself from your reel. Periodically twitch the tip of the rod in order to keep the fly from catching on any rocks along the way. After you have let out 30 yards or so of line, flip over the reel bail and begin your retrieve. Be sure to bring the fly back through the deepest and slowest-moving portions of the river first and reel your line in slowly. Do not forget that your fly will rise up toward the top of the water due to the force of the river's current. You must keep your line speed down to minimize the effect the current has on your fly; you want it to ride a good 6 inches to a foot below the surface. By twitching your rod at regular intervals during your retrieve, you will make your fly act like a wounded minnow, fighting the river in search of shelter.

Playing the Salmon

Regardless of whether you use a fly, a jig, or a lure to hook your salmon, the real struggle comes once you have gotten a strike. Salmon are extraordinarily strong fish, and they swim with great speed. When the kind of force exerted by a fighting salmon comes to bear on your rod, reel, and line, you can be in for some real thrills and some real trouble.

The salmon's first run will be against the pull of your rod, although the fish will sometimes favor a lateral retreat. Always, the fish will be looking for a way to escape the pool where you have hooked it. Most salmon are lost by anglers who were unable to keep up with their fish, and so it may be necessary for you to move quite quickly in the direction in which your fish is escaping. This can be tricky, as the floors of most rivers are slippery and far from level. A pair of waders fitted with felt soles can be very valuable to you here. The felt grips well on rocks, even those covered with moss and slime.

Once your salmon has finished its first run, or even during that primary run, it will jump. There is nothing to beat the sight of a mature salmon taking to the air, its head shaking at your hook in an attempt to wriggle free. There is also very little to match the disappointment of losing your fish at this precise moment. To avoid this, you must drop your rod tip as you feel the fish coming up toward the surface and then bring it carefully back into an upright position once the fish has reentered the water. This motion will allow the fish to take out line as it leaps, taking stress off your line and ensuring that the fish does not break off.

Lake Trout

The lake trout (*Salvelinus namaycush*) is not a leaping fish. In fact, you will probably find that the laker fights much like its close relative the brook trout, by heading down deep and making repeated runs away from your boat. Both the laker and the brookie are members of the char genus, which also includes the Arctic char (*Salvelinus alpinus*), the Dolly Varden (*Salvelinus malma*), the bull trout or inland Dolly Varden (*Salvelinus confluentus*), and a close relative to the laker, the siscowet (*Salvelinus namaycush siscowet*).

Lake trout live in the cold depths of lakes and, like the other chars, avoid waters that run over 65 degrees. This means that good opportunities for catching them near the water's surface come only during the very early and very late parts of the season when surface temperatures are below 60 degrees. During the midsummer, lake trout will dive down 100 feet or more to live in the cooler water.

Nothing can compete with the thrill of fighting a big salmon or laker with ultralight gear.

I have already described fishing for salmon just after the water ices out, trolling lures from a boat right along the surface. Fishing for lakers early in the season, when surface temperatures are just about 45 degrees, is done in the same fashion. However, once those trout have headed down to their summer holding depths, the only way you can follow them is with downriggers.

Downrigger Fishing for Lake Trout

Most successful downrigger anglers set up their reels with either 6- or 8-pound-test line. The amount of line that you will have to let out just to get the lure or fly down to the fish is such that the really light lines will simply snap once you try to set the hook.

Normally, I am not a big fan of swivels, but when you are fishing at great depths and using high-flutter lures like the Mooselook Wobbler, it makes very good sense to do something to prevent your line from getting kinked up. Cut off about 3 feet of line from the end and tie the 3-foot length to one eyelet of the swivel. Then tie the other swivel eyelet to the line still attached to your reel. Finally, tie your lure to the unattached end of the 3-foot length. This will allow the lure to flutter down at its cruising depth without twisting up all the line you have let out.

In terms of tackle selections for lakers, you can use practically the same gear I recommend for salmon. Lakers can grow into the 20- and 30-pound range, and like salmon, they have enormous strength. Unlike the salmon, though, the lake trout is prone to diving as a means of escape, and so you will spend a great deal of your time pumping line up from the bottom, a little at a time. Be sure your reel's drag is properly set before you start out, as it will be getting quite a workout once you hook into a fish.

You will need an accurate depth finder to watch out for the contours of the lake bottom. For obvious reasons, running the heavy weight or cannonball of the downrigger against the bottom can be fairly counterproductive. In fact, not only will it lead to your breaking your line, but it should also scare away every fish in the immediate vicinity. Keep your eyes open to changing slopes, drop-offs, and valleys as they are reported on the depth finder. You will want to change the depth of your line accordingly.

Mooselook Wobblers are one of the best lures to use when fishing for lakers in the deep. Fluorescent-colored streamers also work quite well. You also might try Marabou-type streamer flies like the Black Ghost. On the whole, though, spoon lures like the Wobbler seem to work the best.

Run three or four lines out of your boat at varying depths. A good bet would be to experiment with one set at 10 feet, another at 30, another at 50, and one at 60 or 70 feet. Once you discover at what depth the fish are holding, you can make an adjustment to that level. Keep your speed down at first, maybe 2 to 3 miles per hour, or about the speed of a man walking, so as to give the fish ample opportunity to look over your lure.

Like lake-dwelling salmon, lake trout have a fondness for smelt. Should you pick up a large school of smelt on your depth finder, cruise this area several times. The big lake trout can usually be found at the bottom of the school. Sometimes lakers feed on masses of recently stocked trout as well, and again, you should set your lines so that they pass just under the mass of smaller fish.

Another very effective maneuver, which works well on both lakers and salmon, is to set a zigzag course. While a good fish may be attracted to your lure or fly as it swims past and might even take up the chase at that point, the sudden change of direction which indicates flight can prove to be irresistible for the hungry salmon or lake trout. Try this move out if you pass over a large school of smelt once or twice without getting a strike. If there are any big fish down there, this will get them moving to you.

During the fall, lake trout move out of the depths and into the shallows to spawn. Like all trout, lakers will seek gravel beds to dig out their nests, or redds, and lay their eggs. It is now that these elusive fish are most vulnerable, and they can be taken from canoes and even off the shoreline. Like most spawning fish, lake trout become extremely territorial when mating, and just about any lure will cause a fuss when dragged through their redds. I have had good success with spoon lures like the Phoebe,

Mooselook Wobbler, and Silver Minnow, although I've also taken lakers on top water lures like Rapalas at this time. It's even possible to jig for lake trout with White Marabou jigs.

In any case, I would urge you to release all of your spawning fish. Salmon are also fall spawning, and it just makes good sense to let these fish go about their business once you have successfully boated or landed them during the autumn months. The future of fishing is quite literally in your hands at this time of year.

12

Walleye and Northern Pike

O f the two species to be discussed in this chapter, the more maligned has to be the wallcye (*Stizostedion vitreum*). Related to the perch, the walleye is sometimes mistakenly referred to as the "walleyed pike." True, the walleye does appear to have the head of a northern pike, attached to the body of an oversized perch, and it is also a fact that walleyes can grow to enormous size, just like pike. Also, both spawn in the early spring in the river mouths of the lakes where they live. But when it comes to actually catching the pike and the walleye, the similarities end.

Walleyes

Walleyes are found throughout the northern portion of the United States and are a favorite game fish in Canada. They favor deep, cold water to live in and are therefore quite hard to catch once water temperatures have headed up past 65 degrees. Only by using downriggers and live bait do midsummer walleye anglers encounter much success on the water.

Perhaps the most widely employed method of taking walleyes is the famous Lindy-Rig, a bottom-fishing setup involving a sliding or "walking" weight and a live shiner or night crawler. The weight of the Lindy-Rig alone makes it impractical for use by ultralight anglers, however. Therefore, we must use our wits to take these great fish when they begin their spawning runs.

During the early days of spring, when the cold gray of March has barely begun to give way to the moist promise of April, the walleyes begin to mass around the mouths of major rivers. They begin to head upstream once the water in the rivers reaches about 40 degrees, right as the thermal layer at the bottom of the lake, which sank the previous fall, has begun to "turn." As noted in chapter 10, during the late fall the surface water on most northern lakes eventually chills to 39 degrees,

If you wish to release your walleye and are not using a landing net, pinch your hand around the area immediately behind his eyes, where a neck might appear on another animal. (Photo courtesy Stren Fishing Lines.)

and this water, having become denser than the water under it, will sink to the bottom of the lake. As the lake warms up and the water on the bottom turns warmer and begins to rise, just after the surface has freed itself of ice, the walleyes are on the move.

Once the walleyes move into the comparatively shallow water of the rivers, they become vulnerable to a wide variety of strategies which anglers use to catch them. As mentioned, the use of live bait and heavy 10- and 12-pound-test lines is an extremely successful method. However, if you wish to take walleyes with ultralight spinning gear, you would do well to try the following procedure.

First, spool your reel with a somewhat heavier line than normal. If your pleasure normally runs to 4-pound test, as mine does, you will want to upgrade to 6-pound. You may also want to use a copolymer line like Berkley's TriMax or Bagley's Silver Thread. Copolymers resist abrasion and all the nicks a fighting walleye can dish out as it scrapes along the river bed looking for objects with which to break your line off. These lines are available in extra-clear formula so that you can fish with them during sunny days when the water runs transparent. However, for the most part you will be fishing in stained water filled with the silt and runoff of the spring thaw, making the choice of line color somewhat less of a concern than at other times of the year.

Second, wear the heaviest-duty insulated waders you can find. The water temperature will run in the low to perhaps the mid-40s, making wading very uncomfortable. Neoprene waders can be a good idea, although you can get away with regular rubber waders if you dress warmly underneath them. In either case, plan on getting yourself out of the water for 10 minutes for about every 20 minutes you spend wading and casting. Your legs can become numb from the constant cold of the water, and this can be quite dangerous as you walk along the uneven terrain of the river bottom. A slip under these conditions can lead to tragedy if your legs are not supple enough to react quickly.

Third, bring a net that is large enough to scoop out a fish in the 3- to 6-pound range. There is a favorite story of mine which speaks well of the need for a good net when walleye fishing.

One late April afternoon some years ago, my friend Mike Russo and I were on a large river in north central Vermont, fishing with our ultralight rigs for spawning walleyes. I had been using a ⅙-ounce silver Kastmaster without much success and decided, quite on a lark, to switch to a Number 2 silver Mepps which trailed a bare treble hook. I cast upstream into the current of a small run and let my lure sink for a long 10-second count. I began to reel the line back, keeping my speed in check so that I could feel the blade of the lure engage as it moved along at a speed which kept it barely ahead of the current. My hope was to keep the lure running at a depth of a couple of feet so as to attract the attention of the fish as they moved upstream. After seven or eight casts into the same run, a medium-sized walleye struck, and I pulled the rod tip up sharply to set the hook.

Walleyes do not jump. Instead they will fight along the bottom, darting in a series of short zigzag runs. Most of the time, they will stay down deep, looking to cut your line on the rocks below. A friend of mine once unkindly referred to fighting a walleye as being "like pulling up an old truck tire." I would only point out that truck tires do not strain your reel drag by yanking line off the spool. Also, tires rarely rush you, forcing you to wind line in as fast as your reel and arm will allow.

As my fish began to lose its strength, it floated up onto the surface and listed to one side. I had every intention of keeping this fish, and so I lifted it up out of the water by grasping it underneath its gills. Had I wished to release the walleye, I would have had to take it by pinching my hand around the area immediately behind its eyes, where a neck might appear on another animal. The fish held still as I stumbled back toward shore. I lifted the walleye up high and called over to Mike, who was fishing some distance downstream from me. As he waved his approval, my fish gave a tremendous heave and wrenched itself loose from my grasp.

With a loud splash, the walleye landed on its side in the shallow water at the edge of the river bank. It thrashed about, trying to right itself. In a moment of absolute panic as I watched my fish edge over to the underwater drop-off and certain escape, I did the only thing I could think of doing. I sat on him. To this day, Mike claims he does not really know what happened. One moment he was watching me proudly show off my fish, and the next I was plopped down in the river, seemingly trying to dig a hole under my rear end. The fish was nowhere to be seen. After an agonizing search beneath the seat of my waders, I ascertained that my walleye had indeed escaped. I stood up, my pride completely destroyed, and waded back out into the water.

The happy epilogue to this story is that while a net would certainly have saved me the embarrassment and shame of that moment, I was able to hook into another walleye shortly thereafter, and Mike and I cooked it up that evening over a wood fire. However, the lesson has not been lost on me. A net is your greatest ally when fishing for walleyes. They are simply too large a fish to take by hand with any ease or real grace.

As I have demonstrated, Number 2 Mepps work very well on walleyes, as do silver spoon lures like the Kastmaster, the Fiord, or the Dardevle. You should also try the Silver Minnow, as it has a lively flashing action and is perfect for bouncing along the river bottom. But I think most of the time spent fishing for walleyes should be spent jigging, and that is why I would suggest that you bring along a large number of ⅛-ounce leadhead jigs.

Jigs are fantastically versatile lures, as you read in the chapters on bass and lures. They can be made to imitate a whole

The strategy for fishing spawning pike is very similar to the one you would employ for spawning bass. You should fish from a canoe and quietly work the shoreline of the lake or river mouth you have selected.

range of aquatic life—crawfish, grubs, and leeches. A ⅛-ounce jig head tipped with a long-tailed brown or black grub very effectively imitates a night crawler, one of the most highly prized walleye baits. As with all jigging, the object is to allow your jig to sink to the bottom and then slowly retrieve it, twitching it as it bounces along the rocks and gravel on the river floor or the ledges of a lake drop-off.

Walleyes are most easily caught during the spring when water temperatures are cool and their spawning urge is hot. As they move out of the depths of the lakes they normally inhabit and into the river tributaries where they spawn, they become highly aggressive. It is possible for the lucky ultralight angler to take some truly enormous fish at this time.

Generally, walleyes are caught by casting your lure upstream if you are on a river, or onto the edge of a drop-off if you are fishing a lake. When jigging, your task is to keep that lure down, right near the bottom; you really will not be retrieving your line so much as just keeping up with the slack. If you have selected a spinning lure like a Mepps, you must work your lure through the water so that it stays deep but still appears to be swimming. On a river, you will want to bring the lure back toward you at a speed that is barely faster than the current. On a lake, try to keep the lure down but retrieve fast enough to keep the blade rotating. You will want to keep this same strategy in mind when using spoons: keep it slow, but keep it flashing, too.

The walleye suffers from one great disadvantage. Its popularity as a source of meat has caused its numbers to diminish in various parts of the U.S. In Vermont, for example, the state's largest fishing derby, the Lake Champlain International, forbade the entry of walleyes in the 1993 competition. Walleye catches over the previous five years had been in decline, and the Vermont Fish and Wildlife Department that year also began to clamp down on catches of walleyes during the spring spawning season along Lake Champlain's tributaries. If you plan on doing some walleye fishing, I think it really pays to contact your state Fish and Wildlife Department and ask for their reading on the relative health of the walleye population. Even if you get a glowing report of bountiful waters teeming with walleyes, be restrained in the number of fish you keep.

Northern Pike

I spend most of my time in the summer teaching people how to fly-fish for trout, that particular group of species being my favorite to fish for. However, I grew up on the ocean, and as a small child I would go down into the surf and cast for bluefish. Blues are among the nastiest fish in the water, what with their huge jaws, sharp teeth, and lightning-fast speed. It wasn't until I went fishing one summer in northern Ontario that I discovered the blue's freshwater soul mate, the northern pike (*Esox lucius*).

Evil looking and lethal in their attack, northerns are among the most exciting game fish anywhere. And you can find lots of them scouring the shallows in search of mates during the early spring months, right after lakes have completely iced out. Spawning season for northerns finds them exposing themselves in water that is only a few feet deep as they pair off, dig nests, and lay eggs. They are extremely vulnerable to anglers at this point because they will attack almost anything that strays in front of them. Some of the best lures to work are Mooselook Wobblers, Phoebes, Kastmasters, shallow-diving crankbaits, and live bait. Most folks like to fish for northerns with live shiners, but I prefer to work the edges of weed beds in 3- to 5-foot water with Phoebes or Bagley's Bang-O lures.

For years I have fished for northerns on a small piece of water located in the Champlain Valley of northern Vermont. But in recent seasons the pike fishing has diminished there in favor of the largemouth bass. Not that I have anything against bass—in fact, I think they are a lot of fun. But in late April there is something really thrilling about tying into a good 3-foot-long northern and feeling it pull your canoe around a shallow pond. Then, when the heat turns on in late August each year, I set out to find new pike water to return to the following spring.

One especially hot August morning, my good friend Rob Scharges and I took a drive to a lake to the south of us that neither of us had ever visited before. There was a good boat launch just off the main road, in the southern half of the lake, so Rob and I loaded my canoe with ultralight rigs, lots of crankbaits, jigs, and spinnerbaits and set off at about 7:30 in the morning.

The shoreline of the lake was heavily overgrown with milfoil weed and lily pads. This was a shallow piece of water, and the weeds were a big impediment to fishing. But weeds are also ideal cover for big fish, and we bravely cast into the green goop in search of them.

I was into a good fish pretty quickly, and just as fast, I lost him. I had been using a small black and silver Bagley Bitty-B and had been running it down around 1½ feet below the surface. The fish had grabbed at it angrily and had begun to run instantly when I felt the line go limp, signaling that I had set the hook a fraction of a second too late. As we cruised along the edges of the weed beds, we noticed a deeper, cleared-out channel running the length of the southern end of the lake. We paddled out toward it, keeping the edge of the weed bed within casting range. We were following the shaded edge of an island's shoreline when Rob pulled up hard on the tiny spinnerbait he had been fishing along the bottom of the channel and the line began to scream out.

Northern pike do not normally run too hard after their first big surge. Usually they just hug the bottom until they are brought within sight of your boat or canoe. Rob's pike followed this pattern perfectly, and he grinned when he got his first look at it. But pike also seem to find their greatest strength just when they appear most likely to have given up the fight. Suddenly Rob's fish tore off toward the relative safety of the weed bed, peeling off line until it had completely vanished from sight. After several more minutes of battling the pike, Rob was able to boat it and release it. It had not been the largest pike I had ever seen, but it was large enough for me to know that I would have to come back to this lake to pike-fish again. I would wait, though. I would wait until just after the ice melted the next spring, before the weed beds had a chance to choke the main channel, before the sun heated the air and water up, before anyone else had even considered going out fishing. The northerns would be even more active then, moving up into the shallows to spawn.

Like the walleye, the northern pike spawns when water temperatures are in the frigid zone of between 38 and 45 degrees. At that time, as I have indicated, spoon lures like the Mooselook

Wobbler, Dardevle, Kastmaster, and Silver Minnow work well for northerns. In general, it is preferable to select silver as your color, although I have noticed that on dark, overcast days it sometimes helps if you have a little splash of color on your spoon. Yellow seems to work well. Floating crankbaits are effective, too, and for those of you who like to fish these on the surface, the best selections include Number 7 Rapalas, Rapala's Fat Trap, Bagley's Bang-O lure, and the Rebel Minnow. Spinnerbaits are also worth a try. I like to make up my own spinnerbaits by attaching a Number 1 silver blade to a ⅛-ounce jig head. I usually tip my jig with a 4-inch Mr. Twister grub, selecting the color to fit the cloud cover. If I have a nice bright day, I will choose a dark, earthy color like black, smoke, or gray. On overcast days, I go with white or chartreuse.

The strategy for fishing spawning pike is very similar to the one you would employ for spawning bass. Fish from a canoe and quietly work the shoreline of the lake or river mouth you have selected. Be aware of any underwater structures like dropoffs, weed beds, sunken logs, and gravel deposits, as all of them make ideal hiding places for big pike. Brushy cover along the shoreline is also well suited for northerns, and they will sometimes press right up into it, waiting for unsuspecting baitfish to swim by.

Once your pike is in the boat with you, do not let go of it. The hold shown here will render it relatively helpless so long as you keep pressure on its neck.

One of my favorite pike ponds is fed at the southern end by a small brook and drains into another brook at the northern tip. The fishing for northerns around the mouths of these two streams is excellent during the spring and early summer. In fact, I will often take my canoe right into the brooks themselves and cast the length of both shorelines, snagging bass and northerns while hiding out from the strong winds that whip up across the pond during the middle portion of the day.

Perhaps the greatest challenge of northern-pike fishing is the struggle that occurs right after you set the hook and your fish first begins to run. If you are fishing along a shoreline with dense growth or one that features lots of sunken trees, you must work quickly to bring your canoe free of these obstacles before the pike decides to escape into the natural hiding places they provide. Have your canoeing partner reel in his line and take control of bringing you out into the open water where these impediments will be out of your way. Once your pike gets close to the canoe, though, you will need your partner's help in boating your catch.

There are two safe and accepted methods of boating northerns. The first involves a good-sized landing net. Place the net in the water next to the canoe before the pike has gotten too close to you. This will allow the fish to become used to its presence, avoiding a disastrous last-minute surge that may break off your line if the fish is startled by the net's sudden appearance. Put pressure on your fish and slowly ease it head first into the net opening. Once the head and top half of the fish's body is surrounded by the net, have your partner lift it straight up, and you will have your northern pike.

If you do not have a net, you must be much more careful. Pike have large jaws and very sharp teeth which can inflict a good deal of pain and damage to careless fingers. Fight your fish in close to the canoe and grasp it behind the head, about where its neck would be, then lift straight up and into the canoe. Once your pike is in the boat with you, do not let go of it. The hold you now have on it will render it relatively helpless so long as you keep pressure on its neck. Remove the hook using pliers and get the fish back into the water as quickly as possible. The last thing in the world you want is a live pike thrashing about in the bottom of your canoe. These are big, powerful fish, and they can be very hard to handle should you drop them.

13

Panfish: Sunfish, Crappie, Perch

In almost every freshwater pond or lake I have fished, I have come across one or more of the various species of panfish. These warm-water fish are extremely prolific and can even take over a small piece of water, to the detriment of other species like trout. A healthy pond filled with a variety of warm-water species like bass or pike will contain a ratio of 5 pounds of panfish to every pound of all other game fish combined.

If you happen to live near a small warm-water pond, you are among the luckiest of all people. You are doubly blessed if you own a canoe. Casting to panfish from a canoe with your ultralight and a few tiny, $\frac{1}{16}$-ounce jigs is one of the greatest pleasures an angler can enjoy. Besides small jigs like the Poc' It Hopper by Mr. Twister, which I think is a great panfish rig, there are several other lures that work well on panfish. Devotees of spinning lures will find that Mepps, Rooster Tails, Blue Fox, and Panther Martins are extremely effective. Spoons like the Kastmaster and Sidewinder are great, too. There are even tiny spinnerbaits on the market that will allow you to buzz for your favorite panfish in $\frac{1}{16}$- and $\frac{1}{8}$-ounce sizes.

During the spring spawning season, perch and other panfish become almost comically aggressive. I have caught more sunfish than I care to admit to while fishing for bass with a good-sized,

Number 7 Rapala. If you enjoy good top water action, there are plenty of small plugs that work beautifully on all these fish. One of my favorites is the Bagley Bitty-B. This streamlined little crankbait weighs very little, so you really should not plan on using it when the wind kicks up. Casting under these circumstances is just too difficult, and the size of the lure will also make it tough for you to spot in any kind of chop. But on calm mornings, you can have a lot of fun with the Bitty-B or some of the other smaller crankbaits like Rebel's Teeny Pop-R, Fred Arbogast's Hula Popper, or Rapala's Mini Fat Trap.

Rig your reel with some 2-pound-test, low-diameter line. Fenwick Liteline is very good, as is Stren® Magnathin. Both these lines will offer you remarkable sensitivity, allowing you to feel the lightest of panfish strikes while giving you just enough flexibility to let you fight the somewhat larger fish as well, should you tie into one.

Panfish are the perfect type of fish to learn how to use your ultralight gear on. Because they strike slowly and are prone to multiple strikes on a single bait, you will find them very forgiving of your inexperience while you try to sort out your new kit. I teach folks how to fish for the first time on pieces of water where they will find either brook trout* or panfish, as it improves the likelihood that they will (1) get strikes; (2) catch fish; and (3) decide they enjoy the sport because of (1) and (2).

Sunfish

We will begin by looking at bluegills and pumpkinseeds (*Lepomis macrochirus, L. gibbosus*), two very common varieties of what are sometimes called sunfish or bream. They have fairly poor eyesight and little or no selective instincts when it comes to feeding. In other words, they will strike at almost anything that moves. Like all panfish, they are schooling fish. If you should get a strike by casting at one particular boat dock or shallow sandbar, keep at it. You are apt to get many more strikes in the

---

*See chapter 9 on trout for more information on brook trout. Pay special attention to the references to beaver ponds. Also see my book *Fishing Vermont's Streams and Lakes*, in which there is a chapter on beaver pond brookies and how to catch them.

same location. But remember that because they are schooling fish, bluegills and pumpkinseeds will be on the move as a group; once the school decides to make its retreat, the fishing can get cold in a spot almost as quickly as it seemed to heat up.

As I mentioned, small jigs work beautifully on panfish. A tiny $\frac{1}{16}$- or $\frac{1}{12}$-ounce jig with a small plastic grub will do you fine. If you are making your first cast into a new part of your favorite pond, begin by bouncing your jig along the contours of the bottom. This will remind you of midsummer jigging for smallmouth bass, and you may even happen upon one of these high-jumping game fish in the process. Your next cast should be worked at a medium depth. Allow the jig to sink about halfway down to the bottom and then twitch your rod as you bring in a few feet of line. This will cause the jig to swim upward, then toward you before it slowly drifts back downward again. This erratic motion will draw the fishes' curiosity and can bring several fish out of their nearby schools as they give the jig a closer look.

Bluegills tend to strike quite slowly, gently mouthing and then sucking in the jig in a series of what feel like small taps. Therefore, it is important not to set the hook too hard or too quickly once you feel a strike. In many cases, you will pull your jig right out of the fish's mouth before it has had a chance to really make its attack. Also, do not be too concerned if you should miss a strike. Let the jig free-fall for a second or two and then continue to retrieve it. Many times, the bluegill will pick up the chase just as soon as you start to bring in line again.

Fishing for panfish with spoons is usually done by cruising your lure along the top foot or two of the water's surface. This is most effective should you actually see the fish rising. Spinners are worked in much the same way. Spinnerbaits offer you a bit more flexibility, as you can fish them deep by slowly working them along the bottom, or shallow by quickly retrieving them along the top. When you use a quick retrieve, though, you will notice that the buzz blade will sometimes actually break the surface, causing larger fish like bass or pike to take notice as well. This is especially true during the spring, when panfish, pike, and bass are all spawning and are especially prone to protecting their territorial boundaries.

Crappie

Crappie (genus *Pomoxis*) are the largest of the three major groups of panfish under discussion. Also known as calico bass, these fish have a peculiar, large, transparent jaw area which has earned them the nickname "paper mouth." Crappie can be found in many of the same places as other panfish, although I will promise you that lucking into a school of these large bream is not an everyday event.

I have caught plenty of crappie that ran into the foot-long range—far different from my experience with other panfish, where I have felt myself lucky to catch 10-inchers. Crappie have

If you enjoy good top water action, there are plenty of small plugs that work beautifully on panfish.

been known to top a couple of pounds, and these monsters are really something when you take them on ultralight tackle. I still prefer to stick with 2-pound-test line when fishing for crappie, as they will strike at your lure or jig in the same tapping manner that distinguishes all panfish, and I need that extra sensitivity in the line to know when to set the hook. You can use the exact same lures you would select for bluegill and perch when you go crappie-fishing.

Like all panfish, crappie can be taken from rivers and streams, although you are more likely to find them in ponds and lakes. In general, crappie are not quite as energetic fighters as perch or sunfish. They tend to come up to the surface quickly, making their bulk and extreme breadth less of a factor than they might otherwise be. Interestingly enough, you will find it difficult to tell whether you have a sunfish or a crappie on your line until the fish gets close enough to the surface to be seen. However, I have found that crappie tend to stay deep longer when you find them in streams, putting their size to good use as you battle them. Bluegill, pumpkinseed, and other sunfish will do the same thing when you locate them in a river, and I certainly hope you are lucky enough to do so. It's great fun!

Perch

Both yellow and white perch (*Perca flavescens, Morone americana*) inhabit many of the same types of water where you will find sunfish or crappie. Perch are also schooling fish, but you will never mistake a hit from a perch for any other panfish. Perch absolutely wallop at lures when they strike, feeling like fish quite a bit larger than they may actually be. If you have located a school of good-sized perch, you will want to make sure that you set your hook firmly but gently. Perch, like all panfish, have very small mouths, and it is quite possible to rip the lips off a fish by hitting it too hard. This can be a bit of problem, too, because a foot-long perch is going to feel like an awfully big fish when it hits.

I remember one of the first times I caught a yellow perch on ultralight gear. I was fishing for trout in a large river in

Massachusetts with a good friend when I saw a group of fish rising in the wake of a large boulder out toward the center of the stream. I tossed my lure, a $\frac{1}{12}$-ounce Kastmaster spoon, just upstream from the boulder and let it drift down into the wake. Before I had a chance to begin retrieving line, I felt a tremendous tug, and I set the hook. I expected to see a 14- or 15-inch rainbow trout leap out of the water and was somewhat surprised to see the fish hold underwater and move steadily downstream, turning its body parallel to me to put pressure on my line.

I should have recognized this characteristic panfish run, but I didn't. All panfish take advantage of their broad sides when hooked, using the water as a braking system to oppose your line's pull. When you encounter them in moving water, they will make use of the river's current in the same way. The fish I was fighting also did not zigzag the way a brown trout will when it fights below the water's surface, but again, I was not looking at these telltale signs properly.

When I finally brought my fish close enough to net it, I was astonished to see that it was a 12-inch-long yellow perch, a good-sized representative of the species. My friend had been watching the fight from upstream, and he hurried down to meet me. Upon seeing my catch, he burst out laughing and chided me for stooping to snagging "trash fish" instead of trout. I pointed over to the boulder where I had hooked my perch, and we saw several fish rising there. Foolish pride forgotten, we both waded into the river and began to cast to the perch, which kept us quite active and very happy for the next hour or so before they moved on.

White perch are like their more green-tinged cousins in that they sock at lures and jigs with wild abandon, but they can be found in some very unusual places. A freshwater fish, the white perch can also be found in brackish water. My parents live on the banks of a large pond where I used to fish for white perch as a boy. The pond was fed by a small freshwater brook but was located right next to the Atlantic Ocean. Twice a year, the town would open up a cut in the beach that separated the pond from the ocean, allowing saltwater to mix with the fresh. This allowed for a very unusual mix of aquatic creatures, all living in the same body of water. Sagg Pond was host to white perch and freshwater eels as well as blue-clawed crabs, which are most at home in the sea. Sometimes when the cut was open bluefish and striped bass would work their way into the pond as well. One summer, a seal took up residence in the pond, to the delight of all of us children who fished there. The seal dined on many of the same fish we caught, and in spite of this natural competition, neither side seemed to begrudge the other.

But it was the perch that took most of our attention then. My earliest fishing memories are of casting for them with a small red Dardevle lure with a weed guard on it. I grew to love the taste of perch so much that one summer I built a small corral out of chicken wire and sank it in the shallows near the raft my uncle moored at the edge of the pond, so that after a particularly successful day's fishing I might keep extra fish alive for harvest later on.

Both white and yellow perch respond to a lot of the same lures that sunfish and crappie like. One-eighth-ounce jigs with plastic grubs, small spinners like Mepps or Panther Martins, and plugs like Rapalas work best. While I think there is a noticeable difference in the way white perch taste compared to yellow perch (I really prefer yellow to white), nothing separates them when it comes to how they strike, their lure preferences, or how you should fight them. Even though they actually belong to different families (the yellow perch are of the genus *Perca*, while the white perch are of the genus *Morone* and are more closely related to white bass than to perch), a perch is a perch is a perch when it comes to the way they fight, and both are well worth catching on ultralight gear.

Saltwater Species

I n this chapter, I hope to convince you of two things. The first is quite obvious. Concerning your ultralight rig: as with the well-known credit card endorsed by so many well-paid celebrities, you should never leave home without it. There are simply too many places along your way where the fishing just might be good. I always travel with a four-piece ultralight rod, tight in its aluminum tube, whenever I go on vacation. I have dragged my rod and reel everywhere from Jamaica, to Puerto Rico, even to Rio de Janeiro, and I have always found it worthwhile to have done so.

The second point is that you should definitely try fishing on the ocean with your ultralight rod and reel. The excitement of hooking into an exotic species like the barracuda or a more common one like the bluefish is wildly intensified when you're using light gear. There are a few adjustments you may want to make, however, before venturing out.

Tackle and Lures for Saltwater

As you may have to make long casts into the wind when you are out on the ocean and when you cast from shore into the surf, it makes sense to use a long rod, say 6 to 6½ feet in length. You will also want to upgrade the line you use. As I have mentioned throughout this book, I normally prefer using 4-pound test when fishing for trout, bass, and even pike. I would advise moving up at least to 6-pound- if not 8-pound-test line when you go to the ocean. A small bluefish runs about 5 pounds, and even a young barracuda will hit 3 pounds more often than not. Other popular saltwater game fish like striped bass, weakfish, blackfish, red snapper, yellowtail, redfish, and kingfish can make similar claims on your line, given that they too will normally run in excess of 3 pounds.

A stiff-action rod like the St. Croix Legend is a good choice for this kind of fishing. The Legend comes in 5½- as well as 7-foot lengths and can be broken down into two pieces for easy storage on a plane. The Fenwick Golden Wing is another good selection, as it also breaks down in two and comes in a 6½-foot length. For a little less money, either the Daiwa Procaster SST or Samuri rod is a good bet too.

Shimano, Daiwa, and Quantum all make excellent reels for saltwater use. Shimano's Stradic is one of the best, although their Symetre is a perfectly good, less expensive alternative. Daiwa's SS Tournament series are extremely fine reels, as are Quantum's Hypercast and Abu Garcia's Cardinal Pro Max. Regardless of what reel you decide to use, you must be extremely vigilant about keeping it clean and free of salt residue as well as sand. Make a habit of spraying the reel exterior down with tap water after each use and checking the inner workings for signs of salt buildup. You should also spray inside the reel spool with WD40 from time to time to keep it well lubricated.

You might also consider using a copolymer line like Prime Plus and Berkley's TriMax. As noted in chapter 5, Prime Plus features a sheath that can make up roughly a quarter of the total line's volume, while TriMax is a blend of polymers. Both resist water absorption and corrosion from sea salt. While I have used various light lines on bright, sunny days in the same way I would when fishing for trout on clear-running streams in the summer, it makes good sense to power up if you go fishing on the ocean and take advantage of the technology available to you.

Unlike many saltwater anglers, I prefer to fish without the

benefit of a steel leader. The argument for attaching an 18-inch length of steel wire between your line and the lure is that most saltwater species have extremely sharp teeth and powerful jaws, making it very easy for them to bite through your monofilament or copolymer line. This is quite true. I have had bluefish, weakfish, barracudas, and even striped bass break off by cutting my line with their teeth. But I can also promise you that a good-sized specimen of any of these species will slice through a 30- or 40-pound-test steel leader almost as easily. Also, the leader stands out in sharp contrast to the natural surroundings when you are fishing on bright, sunny days, alerting the fish that something is not quite kosher. This is particularly true when you fish the crystal waters of the Caribbean, where bonefish, barracuda, and redfish are most finicky quarry to begin with. I simply feel that the minimal benefit of a little extra strength offered by a steel leader is not of equal value with the stealth of an almost invisible line.

Lure selection for saltwater will vary, depending on the local species, but there are a few lures that seem to work everywhere on every type of saltwater fish. Spoon lures with a lot of flash and a nice, erratic action are always a good bet. My favorites are made by the Acme Tackle Company of Providence, Rhode Island. These folks make the famous Kastmaster, a lure I can

The bluefish's favorite food is the menhaden, a schooling fish that is easily imitated with the famous Kastmaster spoon lure.

remember using since I was about ten years old on bluefish and striped bass as I fished the beaches of Long Island. Acme also manufactures the Phoebe, which is one of my favorite lures for just about anything that swims. In general, you should take along a selection of spoon lures in the ⅛- to ¼-ounce range in silver, silver/blue, copper, and gold colors.

This does not mean that Acme has a lock on all of the great lures. Spinning lures like the Rooster Tail, Mepps, and Blue Fox are excellent attractors. They combine the flash that is so necessary to catch the eye of saltwater predators with the buzzing noise the blade makes as it spins through the water. Top water lures can also be effective, and Rapala and Bagley make some great ones. You should stick to bright colors when using floating lures, though, or at least use lures with a lot of silver or gold paint on them. Stick to Number 5 top water baits and either Number 1 or Number 2 spinners.

One last but very important point regarding your lures. Most lures made for ultralight gear feature hooks that cannot withstand corrosion by salt water. These hooks have been designed to deteriorate after only a few days of extensive exposure to freshwater, so that a fish that breaks off will not be permanently encumbered by a lure protruding from its jaw. It therefore makes a good deal of sense to either change the hooks on your lures before fishing on the ocean, or to switch all your hooks for ones made out of galvanized steel. Even this specially treated type of hook will wear out under constant exposure to sea water, but it will stand up far better than the conventional hooks made of brass and untreated steel.

Bluefish

Once you are out on the ocean, all this selection and preparation will be worthwhile. I have two species of saltwater fish that I call my favorites for ultralight fishing. The first is my old quarry, the bluefish (*Pomatomus saltatrix*). I've fished for blues ever since I can remember, starting as a kid when my family would spend summers on the east end of Long Island. I had a light-action 6-foot fiberglass rod back then with an old Mitchell reel, and I used to bicycle to the beach every day and cast into the surf for the small snapper blues. These fish are the young-of-the-season bluefish, and they generally weigh 1½ pounds or less. On light tackle, they were as much fun to me then as the mature 15-pound bluefish are today.

The best part of the bluefish season along the northern Atlantic coast from New Jersey to Maine is from June through September, although I have caught blues in this region as early as the first week in May and as late as mid-November. Within the confines of the June-September season, though, there is one stretch that runs through the first three weeks in August that is my favorite time to fish for blues with my ultralight. This is when the mature bluefish finish spawning and return to the shoreline where they will remain until they begin their migration south. At the tail end of this three-week period, the first

A happy angler displays the fruits of a bluefish blitz. When blues go on a feeding frenzy, it is possible to catch several fish in the space of a half-hour or less. (Photo by Martin Andonian.)

snappers make their appearance, and the action for adult and young fish can be fantastic! It should be noted that anglers who live along the Carolina coasts will experience this same activity six to eight weeks earlier, as the blues there perform their spawning ritual during the late spring instead of midsummer.

The adults are usually the first to arrive, and they are best approached by boat. It makes good sense to begin your forays either at the break of day or about two hours before sunset. The sea will tend to be calmer during these two times, making it far easier for you to spot the large schools of fish.

Bluefish are among the ocean's great eaters. Their feeding frenzies are terrible to watch. They will quite literally corral large schools of smaller fish—the favored species being menhaden, silverside minnows, and butterfish—forcing the baitfish to pack together as they become hemmed in by the blues' activity. As you first approach a school of bluefish feeding, you will notice the smaller fish swimming side by side in a tight pack with their dorsal fins sticking out of the water. From time to time, one or more of the baitfish will slap the surface out of fright. These schools can cover enormous amounts of water. I can remember seeing schools several acres in size when I was a boy, although in recent years I believe the largest I have seen have taken up only a single acre of the water's surface. Still, it is an awesome sight. When the bluefish make a surge to attack one corner of the school of bait, the smaller fish will all rush away, causing the surface to erupt in a flurry of fins and water.

Blues find this kind of an offering nearly impossible to resist. When bluefish are feeding, you can almost throw out a bare hook and catch fish on it. Blues have been known to continue to feed long after their bellies are full. They become so excited from killing that they continue to chop their sharp teeth at anything that moves. Bluefish will actually injure each other during these "blitzes," as they are sometimes called, and I have caught blues that bore the scars of unfortunate encounters with other frenzied members of their school.

The key to successful fishing when working a school of blues is your cast. Often, you will have to toss your lure over the breaking waves if you are casting from shore. Be assured, though, that bluefish do like to work close to these breakers, as it allows them to trap schools of bait against the turbulent white-water. Therefore, you need not cast more than a couple dozen feet beyond the backs of the waves to place your lure into the midst of a feeding school of fish. When I was writing my thesis in college in 1979, I spent several months back on Long Island where I had spent summers as a boy fishing with light tackle. There I rediscovered the bluefish, pitching my lures just over the tops of the waves and into the cruising bluefish as they snapped through large schools of silverside minnows.

The important point here is that the fish lie close to the shoreline, making it possible for anglers to reach them, even with ultralight equipment. I also spent a good deal of time visiting the sheltered waters along the northern coast of Long Island's south fork, near Montauk, where I would often find blues feeding just 20 feet offshore. The fishing under these conditions is far easier, as you do not have the heavy surf to contend with as you work your fish in.

Striped Bass and Weakfish

Lest you think that I see ultralight gear applicable only to the blue, I should also point out that fishing for both striped bass (*Morone saxatilis*) and weakfish (*Cynoscion regalis*) is great fun with light gear as well. Neither stripers nor weakfish possess the razor-sharp teeth the bluefish has, so you are far less apt to lose your line and lures to them in that way. However, stripers grow much larger than bluefish; in fact, a 60-pound striper is not all that uncommon a beast, while a 30-pound blue is quite rare.

Both stripers and weakfish respond well to surface poppers, and perhaps you are best off to begin by using them. The Rebel Pop-R Plus is an excellent surface lure to use. It has a concave mouth area that causes a lot of splash as you work it through the water. The trick is to twitch your rod tip regularly as you bring the lure across the surface, making the spray imitate a panicking baitfish. Rapala Jointed Minnows are a good bet, too, as the twisting action the tail makes is a sure attractor for hungry stripers or weakfish.

But by far the best lure for either of these species is a tube. Tube lures are very easy to make yourself. All you need is a long-shanked hook, say a Number 4 size, and a 3-inch section of colored plastic tubing. Tubing can be purchased at any hardware store and cut to the desired length. Look for bright colors like yellow, orange, and blue to catch the fish's eye.

Insert the point of the hook tip into one open end of the tube and turn it so that the shank rests tightly against the tube wall and the point is pointed back in the direction of the opening it came through. Carefully push the hook down into the tube until just the eyelet remains exposed. Next, pull the hook back toward the opening, causing the point to dig into the tube and expose itself. Once the hook barb has poked through the tube, tie the eyelet onto your fishing line and get ready to cast. The tube lure should be fished just under the surface at a fairly good speed. It best imitates the sand eel, a favorite food of the striped bass and the weakfish. This lure also works quite well on blues.

Stripers are not known for their great leaps, nor are weakfish. Sometimes they jump, though, and it can be a very sobering sight indeed. While the world record weakfish is only about 20 pounds, the record striper is 78 pounds! Both species will normally be content to fight you under the surface, but have a care. Their mouths are not as bony as a bluefish's, and it is quite easy to rip the hook out of their jaws once you have set it. This is particularly true of weakfish.

Surf Fishing

Two of the greatest problems you face when surf fishing with light gear for bluefish, striped bass, or any other North Atlantic species are the undertow and the set of the ocean. The undertow is caused by the retreating action the ocean makes after a wave has crashed against the shore. The backwash pulls sharply out to sea and into the next oncoming wave. During this time, anglers who are onto a fish will experience a tugging action on their lines as the undertow sucks their lure and fish back into the waves. This action can put an enormous strain on your fishing line, and you must prepare for it by letting up on the fish as it struggles in the surf. The best way to approach this is to think of the undertow as a predictable, periodic increase in the current. You must also remember that the strength of the undertow intensifies as it draws out. Therefore, you gradually let up the pressure on your fish until you see that the next wave is about to break, at which point you can use the power of the *incoming* wave to your advantage. As your fish is struck by the wave, it will be pushed toward shore, and you can gain line on it.

The set is the direction that the ocean's current pulls the water laterally. Depending on the tide and the prevailing direction of the current, the set will pull water either from left to right or right to left. You can gauge the set on any given beach by throwing a stick into the water just as a wave is breaking and then watching which way the stick floats as the undertow begins to pull it out. You must take this motion of water into consideration as well when you fight your fish, as the set works against you when your fish is out beyond the breakers as well as when it is in the surf. I have lost many fish in the shifting backwash of the surf because I did not adequately react to the changing currents created by the undertow and the set. The strain on my line from the ocean's pull caused it to break, allowing my fish to get away.

Regardless of how the set is moving or how hard the undertow is pulling, it is important to bring your fish through the backwash as quickly as you can manage it. With all the turbulence, cross currents, and wave action, there are just too many ways to lose your fish out there if you dawdle. Most successful surf anglers will fight their fish by letting it run once it has taken the lure and they have set the hook. This allows the fish to move out well beyond the breaking waves before you begin to bring it in. In this way, you can tire your fish out before it comes into the backwash.

Fishing from a Canoe

When not fishing the surf, I like to fish for blues and other saltwater species from a canoe, which is quite easy in the sheltered bays, harbors, and inlets along the coastline. By paddling quietly, you can actually situate yourself right on top of the feeding fish and get a perfect view of all the activity. One of the first things you are bound to notice is how the great mass of baitfish seem to surge when attacked, causing a large space to open out in the middle of the school. I have found that if you cast your lure right in the middle of that opening and begin a slow retrieve after the lure has settled 3 or 4 feet below the surface, you can often get very quick results. This is perfectly logical, too, as your lure becomes a lone, erratically swimming and therefore seemingly injured baitfish.

If you choose to fish in protected inlets, lagoons, and flats, you eliminate the problems caused by backwash, sets, and undertows almost entirely. Most of the fishing I have done in the Caribbean has been in such spots. In the warm water of this ocean, the bluefish is not well known. I have fished for blues in Brazil, in the great surfing waters off Rio, and bluefish are also found through the Gulf of Mexico. But if you fish in the Caribbean, you will come across the second of my two favorite saltwater game fish, the barracuda.

Barracuda

One of my favorite places in the world to fish is Luquillo, a small town located on the northeast shore of the island of Puerto Rico. Only a 30-mile drive to the east from downtown San Juan, on Route 3, Luquillo is famous for its lovely white sand beach and its close proximity to the El Yunquo rain forest, only a 15-minute drive to the south along Highway 191. The beach is a favorite of sunbathers and swimmers, and it can become quite crowded during the peak tourist season in January and February.

However, for the ultralight angler with adventure on his or her mind, the waters at Luquillo offer some truly fabulous opportunities. As you walk along the beach to the east, you will soon reach a point marking the end of the official Luquillo Park area. As you continue to walk east past the point, you will soon come upon a large sandbar which stretches out as far as you can see to the east and out to the north, toward a large reef. Except in a few small channels, this water is rarely more than 4 feet deep and most of it accessible by wading. It is also a habitat teeming with aquatic life.

Mullet can be seen quite frequently as they leap in graceful arcs along the water's surface in their attempts to escape being attacked by any of the many predatory species. Grouper and snappers live in the deeper waters of the channels, while the shallows are filled with smaller baitfish like sardines and needle-fish, and the barracuda that feed on them.

The 'cuda is a greatly misunderstood fish. Partially this is due to its appearance. It is a long, streamlined silver beast that stands out against the turquoise water it lives in. In spite of its evil-looking teeth and fearsome reputation, however, the barracuda rarely attacks unless it's provoked or senses the presence of blood in the water.

Barracuda are quite territorial and have a great love for unusual underwater structures. Scuba divers investigating wrecks often find 'cuda living in and around them, and this is a valuable piece of information for the ultralight angler. When fishing at Luquillo, I have always had my best luck by casting at drop-offs, marker buoys, weed beds, and boat moorings. The fish not only will gravitate toward these places, but they will do

Barracuda, like bluefish, have notoriously sharp teeth and must be handled carefully once landed or boated.

so in fairly large numbers. So, if you locate one barracuda, you are quite apt to find several more in the same place.

One of my most successful trips fishing for barracuda took place in December of 1991. I found four boats moored a short distance offshore in about 6 feet of water. I was using a long, 6½-foot rod and some 5-pound-test Fenwick Liteline. The water was crystal clear, and I had stripped off the Stren® I had been using in favor of the smaller-diameter line. I attached a blue and silver ⅛-ounce Phoebe spoon to the line and cast in the midst of the small cluster of boats. I let the lure sink for three seconds before I began my slow retrieve.

The fish struck almost the instant the lure began to move back toward me, and while I was unable to hold onto it, I was able to get a quick look at it. It was a small barracuda, maybe 1½ feet in length. I pulled in my line and cast out to the same spot. Again, the fish hit after only a few seconds and immediately began to pull out line. It was a strong fish, and it ran several times before I was able to bring it in close. Once it came within view, the barracuda rushed straight at me, forcing me to scramble to one side to get out of its way even as I reeled in the slack. The fish passed within a foot or so of me, and as soon as it was behind me, it turned right around and ran back out toward the four boats. This was a hell of a fight! What made it more remarkable was the fact that my fish was only 1½ feet long. Once I got it turned around after its run out to the boats, the fish soon tired, and I was able to bring it in.

I released my fish and watched as it quickly scooted away to the deeper water in the channel. I checked my lure to see that the hooks had not been bent and placed my next cast right at the spot where I had felt my fish strike. After just a few seconds, I was into another barracuda that treated me to a fight similar to the first. I ended up catching and releasing a total of five barracuda in the space of about an hour without ever having to move from the spot where I stood.

A professional scuba diver I met one night in San Juan while playing blackjack told me that he routinely ran into 4- and 5-foot-long barracuda while spearfishing off the Bermuda coast. He told me that while a 'cuda will be as docile as a family dog when you swim around it looking for something to spear, it can turn to attack almost without warning should you spear a fish or should you be holding a freshly killed fish. The chemicals released from a dead or dying fish as well as the fresh blood excite this predator and can lead to some very nasty confrontations. Similarly, a barracuda is quite dangerous when you are fighting it, and there are numerous reports of anglers' being bitten by hooked 'cudas.

Most of the barracuda I have caught off Luquillo ran in the 18-inch to 2½-foot range. This is not to say that you can only expect to catch fish of this size if you choose to hit the waters off Luquillo with your ultralight gear, however. I spotted one of the largest barracuda I have ever seen as it lazily cruised along the surface of the water, right along the edge of a drop-off near one of my favorite spots on the flats. It ended up measuring around 3½ feet, not a true monster, but big enough to make your heart beat a little faster.

Barracuda, like bluefish, have notoriously sharp teeth and must be handled carefully once landed or boated. In fact, it is often best to fish with someone else when you go after either of these fish, just so you can safely release them. In both cases, you will want to have either a long-nosed hook extractor or a pair of pliers to do the dirty work. Blues and 'cudas are very tough fish, and you will not have to spend much time reviving them once you have placed them back in the water. While you will still want to exercise care when you are dealing with them so close up, remain assured that once they do get their strength back they will be far more interested in getting as far away from you as possible than they will be in exacting revenge. Barracuda are dangerous, though, and you should keep this in mind when you fish for them. In addition to their extremely sharp teeth, they have enormous strength and great speed.

Barracuda are best fished with shiny lures, either colored silver or silver and blue. You should remember that these fish are quite selective and will often turn down anything other than the color they have decided to key in on at that particular moment. I spent three days fishing for 'cudas once, only getting strikes on gold lures for two straight days. On the third day, my gold spoons were completely useless and all my strikes came on bright silver lures.

Once your barracuda has been brought in, you should exhibit the same kind of care you'd use in dealing with a bluefish. In fact, blues are far less predictable than barracuda. Bluefish will often attack moving objects without any visible provocation, and their fury as you work to unhook them can be as hazardous as any feeding frenzy. At all times, keep your fingers away from the jaws of both bluefish and barracuda, and move slowly and carefully when securing them as you take the hook out.

Appendix: Resource Directory

Resources for Ultralight Anglers

The following is a list of manufacturers of ultralight equipment:

Abu-Garcia: 21 Law Drive, Fairfield, NJ 07004

Acme Tackle: 69 Bucklin Street, Providence, RI 02907

Fred Arbogast Company: 313 W. North Street, Akron, OH 44303

Bagley Bait Company: P.O. Box 810, Winter Haven, FL 33882

Berkley: One Berkley Drive, Spirit Lake, IA 51360

Blue Fox Tackle: 645 North Emerson, Cambridge, MN 55008

Daiwa Corp.: 7421 Chapman Avenue, Garden Grove, CA 92641

Eppinger Mfg. Company: 6340 Schaefer, Dearborn, MI 48126

Fenwick: 5242 Argosy Drive, Huntington Beach, CA 92649

Harrison Hoge Industries (Sea Eagle): 200 Wilson Street, Port Jefferson Station, NY 11776

Humminbird: One Humminbird Lane, Eufaula, AL 36027

Bill Lewis Lures: P.O. Box 7959, Alexandria, LA 71306

Luhr-Jensen: P.O. Box 297, Hood River, OR 97031

Mann's Bait Company: 604 State Docks Road, Eufaula, AL 36027

Mepps: c/o Sheldons', Inc., 626 Center Street, Antigo, WI 54409

Mister Twister: P.O. Drawer 996, Minden, LA 71058

Bill Norman Lures: P.O. Box 580, Greenwood, AR 72936

Normark: 1710 East 78th Street, Minneapolis, MN 55423

Pradco: P.O. Box 1587, Fort Smith, AR 72901

St. Croix: P.O. Box 279, Park Falls, WI 54552

Shimano: One Shimano Drive, Irvine, CA 92718

Stowe Canoe: River Road, P.O. Box 207, Stowe, VT 05672

Stren Fishing Lines: c/o Remington Arms Co., Inc., Delle Donne Corporate Center, 1011 Centre Road, Wilmington, DE 19805

Triple Fish Fishing Line: 321 Enterprise Drive, Ocoee, FL 34761

Yakima Bait Company: P.O. Box 310, Granger, WA 98932

Here are some major retailers and catalogue companies that carry many of the products discussed in this book.

Bass Pro: 1935 South Campbell, Springfield, MO 65898

L.L. Bean: Main Street, Freeport, ME 04033 (retail store only)

Cabela's: 812 13th Avenue, Sidney, NE 69160

Cortland: P.O. Box 5588, Cortland, NY 13045

Gander Mountain: P.O. Box 248, Dept. OL793, Wilmot, WI 53192

Streamline: P.O. Box 1218, Waitsfield, VT 05673

Index

Also from the Countryman Press and Backcountry Publications

The Countryman Press and Backcountry Publications, long known for their fine books on the outdoors, offer a range of practical and readable manuals on fish and fishing for sportsmen and women.

Bass Flies, Dick Stewart, $12.95 (paper), $19.95 (hardcover)
Camp and Trail Cooking Techniques, Jim Capossela, $20.00
Fishing Small Streams with a Fly Rod, Charles Meck, $14.95
Fishing Vermont's Streams and Lakes, Peter Cammann, $13.00
Flies in the Water, Fish in the Air, Jim Arnosky, $10.00
Fly-Fishing with Children: A Guide for Parents, Philip Brunquell, $19.00
 (hardcover)
Fly-Tying Tips, Second Edition (revised), Dick Stewart, $11.95
Good Fishing in the Adirondacks, Edited by Dennis Aprill, $15.00
Good Fishing in the Catskills, Jim Capossela, with others, Second
 Edition (revised), $15.00
Good Fishing in Lake Ontario and Its Tributaries, Second Edition,
 revised, Rich Giessuebel, $15.00
Good Fishing in Southern New York and Long Island, Second Edition,
 revised and expanded, Jim Capossela, $16.00
Good Fishing in Western New York, Edited by C. Scott Sampson,
 $15.00
Ice Fishing: A Complete Guide...Basic to Advanced, Jim Capossela,
 $15.00
Michigan Trout Streams: A Fly-Angler's Guide, Bob Linsenman and
 Steve Nevala, $16.00
Pennsylvania Trout Streams and Their Hatches, Second Edition (revised
 and expanded), Charles Meck, $17.00
Trout Streams of Southern Appalachia, Jimmy Jacobs, $17.00
Universal Fly Tying Guide, Second Edition (revised), Dick Stewart,
 $12.95
Virginia Trout Streams, Harry Slone, Second Edition, $15.00

We publish many more guides to canoeing, hiking, walking, bicycling, and ski touring in New England, the Mid-Atlantic states, and the Midwest. Our books are available through bookstores, or they may be ordered directly from the publisher. For shipping and handling costs, to order, or for a complete catalog, please write to The Countryman Press, Inc., P.O. Box 175, Woodstock, VT 05091-0175, or call our toll-free number, (800) 245-4151.